Captivating Classrooms

Captivating Classrooms

Educational Strategies to Enhance Student Engagement

Nicholas D. Young
Christine N. Michael
Jennifer A. Smolinski

ROWMAN & LITTLEFIELD
Lanham • Boulder • New York • London

Published by Rowman & Littlefield
An imprint of The Rowman & Littlefield Publishing Group, Inc.
4501 Forbes Boulevard, Suite 200, Lanham, Maryland 20706
www.rowman.com

6 Tinworth Street, London SE11 5AL

Copyright © 2019 by Nicholas D. Young, Christine N. Michael, and Jennifer A. Smolinski

All rights reserved. No part of this book may be reproduced in any form or by any electronic or mechanical means, including information storage and retrieval systems, without written permission from the publisher, except by a reviewer who may quote passages in a review.

British Library Cataloguing in Publication Information Available

Library of Congress Cataloging-in-Publication Data

Names: Young, Nicholas D., 1967–, author | Michael, Christine N., author. | Smolinski, Jennifer A., 1975–, author.
Title: Captivating classrooms : educational strategies to enhance student engagement / Nicholas D. Young, Christine N. Michael, Jennifer A. Smolinski.
Description: Lanham, Maryland : Rowman & Littlefield [2019] | Includes bibliographical references.
Identifiers: LCCN 2018032961 (print) | LCCN 2018033552 (ebook) | ISBN 9781475843668 (electronic) | ISBN 9781475843644 (cloth : alk. paper) | ISBN 9781475843651 (pbk. : alk. paper)
Subjects: LCSH: Motivation in education. | School improvement programs. | Classroom management.
Classification: LCC LB1065 (ebook) | LCC LB1065 .Y68 2019 (print) | DDC 370.15/4—dc23
LC record available at https://lccn.loc.gov/2018032961

∞ ™ The paper used in this publication meets the minimum requirements of American National Standard for Information Sciences Permanence of Paper for Printed Library Materials, ANSI/NISO Z39.48-1992.

Printed in the United States of America

Contents

Preface		vii
Acknowledgments		xi
1	More Than Motivation: Finding Points of Passion for All Learners	1
2	Inclusive Leadership: An Invitation to All Students	17
3	Mentoring for Maximum Involvement: Making Marginalized Students Mainstream	41
4	Reinventing Reading: Making Literacy Instruction Come Alive	71
5	Instructional Practices That Make a Difference: Engaging Students in the Classroom	99
6	Ensuring That All Students Receive Support: A Spotlight on Special Education, At-Risk, and ELL Programs	117
References		133
About the Authors		145

Preface

Captivating Classrooms: Educational Strategies to Enhance Student Engagement is written for school leaders, teachers, and support staff, as well as for parents of P–12 students, aspiring educators, and higher-education faculty who prepare preservice teachers and administrators. This is a book for those who are committed to seeing all P–12 students succeed through active involvement in their own education. While this book largely focuses on understanding the role student engagement plays in education, it does so with an acute awareness that there are myriad factors that influence each individual's engagement and motivation to learn.

Much has been written about the academic and cognitive aspects of students' educational attainment, and those are discussed here in chapters on teaching strategies, literacy, and motivation. However, this book also acknowledges the incredibly important nature of emotional, social, and relational elements of education as they relate to engaged learning, so other chapters cover such topics as student leadership and mentoring.

The motivation for writing this book comes from several concerns:

- Our belief that all students' socioemotional needs should be at the forefront of teaching and learning
- Our observation of the troubling numbers of students who are not fulfilling their academic, social, and career potentials
- Our understanding that levels of anxiety, depression, social aggression, and other mental health problems are rising, both in society in general and in our schools in particular

- Our knowledge that the development of healthy prosocial skills in students with learning disabilities may require different strategies and materials than those for nondisabled students
- Our awareness that promoting positive mental health and academic success increases the likelihood that students will thrive in both arenas
- Our years of educating parents, teachers, school counselors, and other helping professionals, which has led us to recognize that age-specific knowledge can assist these key partners in building students' resilience and self-advocacy
- Our interest in identifying and sharing best practices that lead to academic, personal, and mental health, as well as social success for all students

If it indeed takes a village to raise a child, then it takes a true learning community to educate him or her in a wholistic fashion.

Parents, teachers, and others involved in the lives of students often struggle with the delicate balance of encouraging a greater sense of autonomy and independence and inculcating the skills, values, and attitudes they prize before they launch their children into young adulthood. This is no less true of those who support students with learning struggles, and the challenges are even greater as the support systems so carefully constructed in P–12 settings give way to the greater independence of a college campus or independent living.

Moving from adolescence into young adulthood is a time of many transitions, and secondary school students trying to navigate it may have difficulty. By recognizing the nature of this developmental period, educators, caregivers, and other helping professionals can promote prosocial development. Building students' sense of efficacy by helping them to improve their learning skills and offering them opportunities to work through developmental issues and personal challenges prior to graduating from high school are things that all of us can do. Creating a strong cadre of students who can persist to graduation requires school, community, and home commitment.

The concerns noted here are the focal points of the chapters of this book. We balance theory, research, and data-driven best practice as we depict the socioemotional and mental health tasks that students (especially those with any sort of learning challenge) face, as well as the strategies that may assist them. Written by an experienced team of higher-education professionals, one of whom also is an experienced public school superintendent and educational leader, this text adds to the growing body of literature on the importance of and approaches to promoting student engagement by marrying the social, emotional, mental health, and transitional components of the P–12 spectrum.

Providing a foundational understanding of some of the salient issues facing students today, we hope to empower all those working to ensure student success by illuminating the particular challenges that they and their families may face. We share strategies and best practices for enhancing students' academic success, creativity, resiliency, prosocial behavior, and positive mental health. As a practitioner-oriented text, this book offers a truncated review of relevant literature, followed by suggestions for guiding practice.

It is our hope that all who occupy powerful places in the education and development of students will find valuable strategies to augment their knowledge base, skills, attitudes, and habits within the following pages. In the final analysis, we, the authors of this book, join our fellow educators and parents in the struggle to do all we can to more fully engage the next generation in the important task of learning the skills and knowledge necessary for a successful and fulfilling career and life.

Acknowledgments

Our deepest appreciation and heartfelt thanks to Sue Clark for her expert editorial assistance and personal friendship and support. We are forever grateful for her substantial contributions to this book. Even more so, we consider her a valued friend.

Chapter One

More Than Motivation

Finding Points of Passion for All Learners

In research conducted by Wolpert-Gawron (2018), students identified what they themselves felt were the necessary components to spark their engagement in learning. What Wolpert-Gawron found was more than just motivation:

> A classroom that is focused just as much on engagement as it is on academic achievement not only runs smoother, but also achieves an overall goal that should function as a teacher's target . . . developing people who appreciate lifelong learning. After all, enjoying school doesn't end when our students leave our schools' walls. The joy of learning should be a cushion that carries students into higher education and beyond. (p. 2)

For this reason, she argues that the very elements that engage students in deep learning also help teachers remain passionate about their craft.

What drew teachers to the profession was a desire to spark excitement in their students, to make learning meaningful, to affect lives both in the classroom and beyond. Taking it one step further, engaged teaching, which stimulates student engagement, cannot be based solely on the power of a teacher's personality but is a combination of personality and pedagogy (Wolpert-Gawron, 2018).

Using a one-question survey, students were asked to name the key ingredient to an engaged learning experience. Interestingly, despite differences in age, nine themes emerged that are as true today as they were when Wolpert-

Gawron began the poll in 2011. They include a desire to work together, more visual learning, connecting the learning to real-world experiences, movement in the classroom, work choices, mixing up the learning, students seeing teachers as humans, creating something in a new way, and final projects instead of assessments (Wolpert-Gawron, 2018). Before moving to a discussion of these key factors, it is important to understand human motivation.

MOTIVATION DEFINED

Motivation may be defined as the "energy that human beings direct toward achieving a goal" (Ginsberg, 2015, p. 2). When a student can see that what is being learned makes sense and is important in terms of values and goals, motivation is high (Ginsberg, 2015). One important factor in engaged learning is the source of motivation: intrinsic or extrinsic. Intrinsic motivation "reflects the positive potential of human nature . . . , the inherent tendency to seek out novelty and challenges, to extend one's capacities, to explore, and to learn" (Ryan & Deci, 2000, p. 70). Emphasizing the intrinsic aspirations of each student improves his or her self-esteem and self-actualization, whereas heavy emphasis on extrinsic aspirations results in the opposite. Intrinsic motivation involves doing something for the internal sense of pleasure and reward, whereas extrinsic motivation applies to performing in order to earn an external reward (Ryan & Deci, 2000). In order for students to be truly motivated, they must feel that an activity is valuable; that they have the self-efficacy to perform well; or that it will have an outcome that is worthwhile, even if the task is difficult.

Individuals who are *externally regulated* behave in ways that are geared toward obtaining a reward or avoiding a punishment (Niemiec & Ryan, 2009). If the external controls over the behavior are removed, however, one can expect to see a decrease in the individual's behaviors. External regulations are derived from sources outside of the self, and the individual, therefore, has an external locus of control. An internal locus of control allows individuals to accept that their successes can be attributed to their hard work and own failures but with a sense that they can affect more positive outcomes in the future.

Ginsberg decries the frequent use of extrinsic motivations (the proverbial carrot and stick) in contemporary education. Grades, pizza parties, and even candy are used in many classrooms to exert influence on students to become or remain academically engaged. With an intrinsic approach to learning, students engage in learning without rewards. They often experience a loss of the sense of time and feel "flow," in which they are one with the learning task. They are at peak concentration as they value the learning outcome, and they dig more deeply into the subject matter at hand. Ginsberg (2015) notes that students often feel a sense of efficacy, creativity, and even joy—states that lead them to develop lifelong learning habits. Essentially, the opposite occurs with extrinsic orientations to learning.

There are, however, many external controls in school systems that can stymie the motivation of individual students (Ginsberg, 2015). These could be requirements and limitations placed on curriculum, classroom environments, instructional strategies, and means of assessing what students know. In the end, these can have a deleterious effect on student motivation, esteem, and sense of self-efficacy.

Reeve argues that the classroom environment heavily influences student motivation and teachers should support student autonomy and self-determination in the learning process, thus improving the teacher–student relationship. To maximize this supportive environment, teachers must be clear in communicating classroom management and learning expectations, acknowledge and value student perspectives, strengthen students' inner motivational resources, and display authenticity in their interactions with the classroom community (Ginsberg, 2015; Reeve, 2006; Wolpert-Gawron, 2018).

When students and teachers are more motivated and engaged, an autonomy-supportive environment is often present, and their basic needs of competence, autonomy, and relatedness are met. Ginsberg (2015) argues that teachers do not actually motivate their students, as students have innate motivation; however, educators can go a long way in influencing, encouraging, and inspiring students to apply their motivation to positive academic and personal goals.

WHAT MOTIVATES STUDENTS

Integrate Cooperative Learning in Lessons

Wolpert-Gawron (2018) found that integrating cooperative learning was the most frequent answer among all of her student engagement surveys. Researchers concur that cooperative and group learning opportunities benefit learners of all types (Barron & Darling-Hammond, 2008; Johnson & Johnson, 2004; Marzano & Pickering, 2011; Slavin, 1996). There are several main reasons that cooperative learning increases both motivation to learn and academic achievement.

Group motivation to succeed was one of the main reasons listed, as this can pull along reluctant learners or those who do not have a sense of self-efficacy when approaching the learning task. In the best-functioning groups, there also is an intrinsic motivation that comes from caring about the success of other group members (Johnson & Johnson, 2004; Marzano & Pickering, 2011). When this occurs, there is both maximum commitment to the task and emotional support of other learners, which strengthens social bonds and emotional intelligence.

The diversity within a group, through learning styles, preferences, and culture, can help a student see different ways of understanding a concept or various avenues for solving a problem (Celli & Young, 2014). It is as though group members have individual pieces of the puzzle that they can contribute to the whole image.

Wolpert-Gawron mentions the need for doing some preparation work with students so that they have the tools to make the group run successfully and equitably. Spelling out various roles that need to be fulfilled within a group, such as reporter, timer, recorder, and artist, stresses facilitative skills and roles to address the inevitable power dynamics. Assigning or having tasks chosen by students identifies each person's unique contributions, so that each student senses the importance of his or her personal task to the successful completion of the group task. This helps the teacher assess each student in different domains of achievement, including communications skills, content knowledge, collaborative ability, and even leadership potential (Wolpert-Gawron, 2018).

There are also many student-friendly group skills instructions that can be provided. These include how to manage conflict, ensure that all voices in a group are heard, brainstorm and come to a consensus, and keep the group on track toward end goals. Johnson, Johnson, and Holubec (2008) provide a rationale for greater cooperative learning within classrooms, as student–student interaction has historically been undervalued. They argue in favor of a cooperative situation rather than a competitive one, so that psychological health is promoted through relationships with others to achieve collective goals.

A number of different collaborative learning configurations are bound by the common goal of working collectively to achieve ends that benefit both the individual members and the total group: formal cooperative learning, informal or ad hoc groups, cooperative base groups (long-term groups with stable membership), and an integrated use of all three types. There is extensive research on psychological health and social interdependence to boost the use of cooperative learning in the classroom. Cooperative or collaborative learning can't take place in a vacuum; simply putting students together does not guarantee that learning will take place. Teachers must understand how to structure positive interdependence, teach effective collaboration and social skills, develop ways to hold individual students accountable, and promote group processing techniques that are effective in learning situations (Johnson, Johnson, & Holubec, 2008).

Students in Wolpert-Gawron's (2018) surveys proved the power of classroom community—the byproduct of collaborative learning and social interactions—within their four walls, as students engaged as learners within a community that felt like family, and "[i]n fact, many said that without a community in the classroom, they couldn't learn. Sure, they could memorize, but they couldn't or wouldn't participate" (p. 26).

Make Learning More Concrete, Visual, and Technologically Enhanced

It would come as no surprise to most veteran teachers that the vast majority of students in their classrooms are visual learners, many with kinesthetic tendencies, as well. Equally as evident, contemporary students are very tech savvy, used to accessing information through multiple media, and prone to communicating through social media (Young, Jean, & Quayson, 2017). Engaged educators can fight this growing trend or find meaningful ways to incorporate it into classroom learning.

Technology, according to the survey respondents in Wolpert-Gawron's (2018) research, provided students with many more visuals than traditional teaching did. In addition, the students stressed that technology helped them be more independent learners, made them feel comfortable within academic settings, and prepared them well for future endeavors. Both the consumption of content and the creation of it are part of the process of embedding technology in the classroom.

Shabiralyani, Hasan, Hamad, and Iqbal (2015) researched the use of visual aids in teaching and found that they stimulate thinking and improve retention, as well as break up monotonous classroom environments. It is recommended that teachers pay attention to students' opinions as to which visual aids are most helpful in their understanding of content (Shabiralyani et al.,

2015). Many teachers need to receive training or refresher courses to become effective with newer materials, software packages, and methods for meaningful integration of such aids in regular classroom teaching (Young , Jean, & Quayson 2017).

Help Students Discover a Sense of Purpose

Students become more motivated learners when they have a clear sense of their life goals, aspirations, talents, and passions. Even at early ages, children know what they love to learn about, and when there is joy in their learning, there is little need to motivate them extrinsically. Finding one's purpose should lie at the heart of meaningful education. Cook-Deegan (2016) describes purpose as the desire to accomplish something of personal and global importance and cites Bronk's (2011) four components of purpose: dedicated commitment, personal meaningfulness, goal directedness, and goals larger than the self.

Saying that most contemporary American schools are not organized to promote these components, Cook-Deegan instead argues for a purpose-learning curriculum. Though originally centered on a high school curriculum, it is easy to see how elements of this curriculum could be infused into elementary and middle school, as well. The first step is to prioritize internal motivation over external achievement. Intrinsic motivation comes from taking part in learning for which students have a deep internal interest, and their pleasure in this learning is derived from the process itself, not from external rewards (Cook-Deegan, 2016).

Cook-Deegan (2016) also stresses the need for collaboration over competition. Part of a sense of purpose is having a vision that is bigger than the self; thus, students need to have opportunities to develop skills and attitudes that are relevant to today's workplace and to civic engagement (Bronk, 2011). These involve teamwork and collaboration, as well as caring about others' success.

A sense of purpose can emanate from what Bronk (2011) calls "purpose seeking" opportunities. These have at least one of three components that push students outside of their comfort zones and into life exploration: a life crisis, serving others in a meaningful way, or changes in life circumstances. Expanding the curriculum outside of the classroom to include chances for travel, service learning, or community-based projects of interest permits a connection between what one does as classroom learning and its relationship to real life.

All of the aforementioned promote a sense of what Cook-Deegan (2016) describes as "whyness." Rather than working hard without knowing why or not working hard because they cannot see why it matters, students connect academics with purpose. A purpose-based curriculum allows students to create a vision for their future world and see how their academic work can help them achieve that vision.

Help Students Find the Passion in Purpose

Purpose and passion are equal partners in helping students find meaning in life and learning. A role of engaged learning is to help students identify those passions and discover venues for their expression within the broader educational framework. Elias (2013b) notes that students' strengths and passions are rarely hidden in a traditional sense; instead they are hidden by lack of opportunity to put them on display. With a tendency to see education as remediation of deficits, Elias argues for beginning with a strengths- or assets-based approach to each student's learning profile.

From there, teachers can use both formal means, such as inventories or writing exercises, or informal discussions in advisories, home rooms, or one-to-one meetings to have students identify and share hobbies and activities that they love to do and feel that they are good at doing. Elias (2013b) encourages the development of short interviews or other activities that can be done with family to find out about hidden talents. These could be hobbies or aspirations held at previous times that the student may have given up, voluntarily or not.

Students also can make scrapbooks, artwork, or digital displays to share. Elias (2013b) writes of regular independent projects based on interests or multiple intelligences strengths that bring together multigrade groupings of students. The best of these group projects have clear links to academic curriculum yet are born out of student interests and thus are self-motivating.

Research on purposeful individuals shows that they usually had at least three "Spark Coaches"—individuals who took an interest in their passions in school or elsewhere. Teachers must be trained to be spark coaches, but other individuals, such as community mentors or older students, can also fill this role (Cook-Deegan, 2016).

Be Authentic as Teachers

All education is relational, and students cannot have genuine relationships with their teachers unless teachers themselves are passionate, genuine, and engaged with the content they are teaching. Wolpert-Gawron's (2018) respondents asked their teachers to display their own enthusiasm for the subjects they teach, show genuine caring for their students and their achievements, laugh and have a sense of humor, tell personal stories that are related to content to be learned, and talk about their own failures and how they overcame challenges. Palmer (2007) paints the portrait of authentic teachers in relational classrooms as those who

> join self, subject, and students in the fabric of life because they teach from an integral and undivided self; they manifest in their own lives, and evoke in their students, a "capacity for connectedness." They are able to weave a complex web of connections between themselves, their subjects, and their students, so that students can learn to weave a world for themselves. The methods used by these weavers vary widely: lectures, Socratic dialogues, laboratory experiments, collaborative problem solving, creative chaos. The connections made by good teachers are held not in their methods but in their hearts, meaning heart in its ancient sense, the place where intellect and emotion and spirit and will converge in the human self. (p. 3)

Palmer also illuminates the notion of teaching as a human enterprise, rather than a mastery of technique, curriculum, or strategy because

> good teaching cannot be reduced to technique; good teaching comes from the identity and integrity of the teacher. In every class I teach, my ability to connect with my students, and to connect them with the subject, depends less on the methods I use than on the degree to which I know and trust my selfhood—and am willing to make it available and vulnerable in the service of learning. (p. 2)

Palmer's observations reinforce the notion that, without meaningful human relationships—teacher to student and student to student—classroom communities are not formed, and without community, students are far less likely to engage in the hard work of learning.

Use Variety in the Classroom

Students stress the need for variety, as in the following quote: "I also feel engaged when a teacher does something different every couple times we do it. It is so boring when we do the same thing over and over again" (Wolpert-Gawron, 2018, p. 191). Imploring teachers to mix things up, students want classroom teachers to have many different strategies and to use them widely, so that day-to-day learning is somewhat unpredictable in nature.

Students are not simply engaged when materials are presented in ways that match their favorite learning styles and their strongest "intelligences." All students have some aptitude in each of the these, so the mix and match of presentation and assessment styles ensures that they will sometimes be working within their preferred modes and other times will be challenged to "stretch" (Celli & Young, 2014).

Differentiating instruction provides many paths to comprehension of a lesson, but without mixing them up, even effective methods get boring. Students thrive and become engaged by a good challenge, as long as appropriate supports are in place (Celli & Young, 2014). High expectations mean that all learners are expected to master the material in engaging classrooms. This is accomplished through educational planning that assumes all students are smart and that learner potential far exceeds their belief in themselves (Tomlinson, 2015). These concepts provide a sound and solid base for a growth mind-set to take hold.

Have Students Create Products from What They Have Learned

Hands-on learning and creating something with the knowledge they have gained were valued by students in Wolpert-Gawron's (2018) surveys. Students, she found, were most engaged when they were creating something, which is at the top of both Bloom's taxonomy (Anderson & Krathwohl, 2001) and Maslow's (2013) pyramid. As one of Wolpert-Gawron's respondents said, "making the stuff or doing something instead of just sitting and listening is what makes me excited about a class" (p. 158).

Although lecture-style teaching and learning had been the norm, as far back as Dewey (1963), the education of children was believed to be best served through experiential learning. This is clearly seen in the classrooms of today "because our world has changed and requires students to emerge from our schools ready to think, create, and own their own learning" (Wolpert-Gawron, 2018, p. 160). Science, technology, engineering, and math (STEM) classes seem to have adopted the creation approach; however, other disciplines and subject areas lag behind. Using technology is an excellent way to create a final project, and an example might be to develop a promotional campaign, create a public service announcement, build lessons that teach others about a topic, or present a short speech (Wolpert-Gawron, 2018).

Provide Opportunities to Make Choices

Permitting meaningful opportunities for students to make choices in the classroom is one of the primary engagement strategies. It allows students to identify and pursue their passions, learn what their assets are, and—as they progress in their education—begin to translate these findings into possible postsecondary paths. As Wolpert-Gowron (2018) found, student choice builds ownership in learning, allows students to demonstrate learning in the ways that best capture their knowledge, and "enforces true differentiation" (p. 112). Students will become motivated to explore any topic, even one about which they are initially unenthused, by encouraging their input and options.

Bray (2012) urges teachers to go beyond project-based learning to personalize the experience so that students have voice and choice in a project's design and process. Techniques for moving students to ownership of their learning include determining in small groups what students know about the topic and then reporting out to the larger group, using media or personal stories to introduce the topic and then sharing how the topic would traditionally be taught. The teacher then invites the students to redesign the topic to maximize engagement. Other strategies to engage students in curricular choices include explicit teaching in how to brainstorm questions, using large group techniques, and using online resources and software in which students simultaneously share and work on documents (Bray, 2012).

Educators may teach students to use "how" and "why" questions or break big questions into smaller questions that take the big questions deeper. Working in pairs, small groups, or affinity groups, students write and share proposals about how they will explore the questions and receive feedback as they progress (Bray, 2012). With the students driving the learning process, the teacher's role becomes that of guide, facilitator, and resource provider, allowing the students to own responsibility for moving toward answers to their driving questions (Larmer, 2016).

Larmer feels that student choice is essential in the twenty-first century, as the world is faced with increasingly complex problems and needs active leaders and problem solvers to tackle them. Student choice and voice provide an early education in those tools of citizenry; however, there are some cautions when creating a more engaging classroom (Alber, 2014). Teachers should, for example, be able to clearly articulate the purpose for giving students voice in a project and sometimes limit choices (Larmer, 2016).

Students also need scaffolding and structure as they build their way to being confident in academic choices. This might include having a list to choose from initially, before moving to self-generated topics. Students may take a survey at the beginning of the year to develop that list of possible topics from their interests. Larmer (2016) also argues for the inclusion of student voice at the end of projects, building reflection into the conclusion. This allows students to evaluate different phases of their work and identify strategies that might improve the process in the future.

Democratic classrooms as not only more engaging but also capable of preparing students for a world of the future rather than the present. This comes from shaking up the "deep structures" (Morrison, 2008, p. 57) of most schools that posit that knowledge comes from outside human mediation and construction. By showing students that knowledge emanates from their passionate questions and that they are the co-constructers of knowledge through some of the processes described earlier, teachers can cultivate a next generation of learners who are excited to tackle hard questions and who have a sense of the things that captivate them the most.

Make Real-World Connections

As Wolpert-Gawron's (2018) student surveys demonstrate, real-world connections motivate students to embrace the necessity of learning even seemingly uninteresting things. This is further supported by Wilhelm, who states, "We aren't in the business of preparing our students to take tests for the rest of their lives. We aren't in the business of helping our students learn to navigate school as an end-all, be-all model of life's journey. . . . We're in this to develop tools to use in the real world" (cited in Wolpert-Gawron, 2018, p. 74).

What often appears as students' lack of motivation for a learning activity may actually be a lack of understanding of why certain knowledge or skills are useful, relevant, or imperative for real-world success or survival (Wolpert-Gawron, 2018). It is the teacher's role to provide the connections that are not easily visible to his or her students in order to lay a foundation for motivation to undertake a learning project.

Strategies for making real-world connections an everyday part of classroom learning include inviting outside experts into the classroom to talk about how they use the content of the project in their everyday lives, promoting authentic audiences to assess projects, and drawing on the exhibition of concepts (McDonald, Smith, Turner, Finney, & Barton, 1993; Wolpert-Gawron, 2018). Yet another strategy is to derive driving questions for project-based learning from current local, national, and global situations; Wolpert-Gowan describes these as "what's going on in current events, what's happened in the past, and what connects to the students themselves" (p. 88). Also stressed is the interconnectedness of all knowledge by desegregating the content areas, noting that, in real life, subject areas blend into each other and rarely stand alone as separate silos of content (Wolpert-Gawron, 2018).

Use Kinesthetic Learning

Students, particularly boys, mentioned that they need to move around in order to learn (Wolpert-Gawron, 2018). Movement of the body engages not only those who are more kinesthetic in their learning preferences but also all students (Celli & Young, 2014). Exercise and movement increase blood and oxygen to the brain, lower stress, and add to new neuron growth (Jensen, 2005; Rhodes, 2015).

Evidence suggests that stress is a significant factor in creativity, memory, behavior, and learning, says Jensen (2005), regularly cited as the father of brain-based learning and teaching. Teachers who intentionally manage stress factors (purposefully decrease or increase stress) in their classes are more likely to create a positive classroom environment. Among the many ways to decrease stress in the classroom are integrating movement and stretching exercises, incorporating recess, teaching coping skills, practicing mindfulness and meditation, and using physical education.

Moderate glucose levels boost memory making and can be maintained through food, stimulating emotions, and physical activity. Savvy teachers manage their instructional strategies so that their students can better maintain moderate glucose levels to help students form stronger memories (Jensen, 2005).

No matter how much students memorize, recite, and study, muscle memory is always greater than brain alone (Sinha, 2014). The use of kinesthetic learning in the STEM areas is important, and there is a strong connection between these subjects and creativity. As an example, movement revolutionizes how we think about teaching subjects like math (Major, 2016; Sinha,

2014). Movement is a learning style and should be encouraged; breaking lessons into shorter, activity-based segments and introducing appropriate props to manipulate during lessons increases movement (Major, 2016).

Teach in Culturally Responsive Ways

Ginsberg describes the incredible diversity found in contemporary American classrooms. Motivation and culture are inextricably linked, as such feelings as safety, belonging, and respect inside and outside of the classroom form the basis of academic motivation; however, because "misconceptions abound on matters of will and purpose, especially when culture, ethnicity, language, life experience, and orientation towards learning markedly vary among students and between students and educators," teachers must intentionally create culturally responsive classrooms that motivate all students (Ginsberg, 2015, p. 3).

There are four conditions of the motivation framework for culturally responsive teaching that both mirror and integrate many of the topics discussed previously in this chapter. The first condition is establishing inclusion, and the criteria are respect and connectedness (Ginsberg, 2015). Teachers must ponder the question of how they will create a learning environment in which students and teachers feel respected by and connected to each other. The second condition is developing a positive attitude. The criteria here are choice and personal relevance. In creating this condition, teachers must think about how they will give students choices and orient learning toward personal cultural relevance for different students. Enhancing meaning is the third condition, and it involves the creation of engaging and challenging learning experiences that are centered on students' perspectives and their relationship to civic responsibility. The criteria for this condition include challenge and engagement. Finally, teachers must consider competence, as Ginsberg asks, "[H]ow does a particular learning experience create a shared experience that students have effectively and authentically learned something they value?" (p. 27). The four conditions work together to develop intrinsic motivation within diverse student populations by promoting learning environments that stress challenge and engagement yet provide safety, unity, respect, and support among all classroom members. Similar to Maslow (2013), Ginsberg argues that no learner will challenge him- or herself to engage fully in learning (self-actualization) without feelings of safety, belonging, and healthy self-esteem.

How each student makes sense of the world and constructs meaning is very much culturally bound. Ginsberg (2015) argues that our values, perspectives, and emotions are socialized through culture, which she defines as the "deeply learned confluence of language, values, beliefs and behaviors" (p. 3). To create a culturally responsive classroom and curriculum, teachers must introduce all students to the concept of culture and then follow up with exercises and activities that permit students to personalize that concept, share strengths and backgrounds, and create a strong sense of community based on valuing each individual's assets and heritage.

Recognizing that most teachers carry huge loads of students each semester, especially at the secondary level, coming to know the backgrounds, strengths, and aspirations of each student is a daunting task, yet creating curriculum and experiences that regularly allow students to study in ways that are meaningful to them can elicit much about individual profiles and cultural components of learning (Ginsberg, 2015).

FINAL THOUGHTS

Students themselves are the best source for understanding what motivates them to become engaged in the learning process. It appears that there are common threads that run through the fabric of engaged learning. Among these are the importance of student voice and choice, relationships between and among students and their peers and students and teachers, and the need for safe and supportive learning communities. Students also crave stimulating classrooms that meet multiple intelligences, allow for movement and collaborative learning, and use technology and visual aids to reinforce learning.

Students also need to know the relevance of what they are learning—how it connects to the real world and how it can be used creatively. Engagement comes from individual passions and goals, and when those are tapped, students are intrinsically motivated to work hard, challenge themselves, and step outside their comfort zones.

Intrinsic motivation theory undergirds the best teaching and applies to all students, across all cultures. Deliberately cultivating classroom environments, curriculum, and communities in which there is intrinsic motivation to learn is the surest way to create lifelong learners and engaged citizens. As Ginsberg (2015) notes in her epilogue, "When people feel respected and connected in a learning environment, when people endorse or determine learning they find relevant, and when people engage in challenging and authentic experiences that enhance their effectiveness in what they value, people learn" (p. 241).

POINTS TO REMEMBER

- Students are very clear about the seminal factors that engage them in the classroom and keep them engaged. These factors fall into several categories: relational, instructional, aspirational, and creative.
- Students need opportunities to work collaboratively, to move freely, and to make choices in their academic lives.
- Students need genuine teachers who are not afraid to teach from the heart, share personal experiences, and serve as "spark coaches" in drawing out and nurturing students' talents.
- Intrinsic motivation is at the center of all genuine learning.
- In order for students to thrive, classroom communities must meet such basic human needs as safety, belonging, and a healthy self-esteem; teachers must create these conditions intentionally with the class.
- Although it is impossible for any teacher to meet every student's preferred learning styles, cultural styles, and multiple intelligences profile at all times, savvy teachers prepare their classrooms and curriculum with diversity in mind.

Chapter Two

Inclusive Leadership

An Invitation to All Students

A CASE STUDY

In 2001, Wadleigh Secondary School, located on 114th Street in central Harlem, was a failing school in all respects. On a good day, 70 percent of its students showed up for school. Only one-half of these students were graduating; a scant 25 percent of Wadleigh's grads were headed to college (Newcomb & Michael, 2010). There were discussions among the chancellor's cabinet about shutting Wadleigh's doors permanently—a tragedy for a school that a generation earlier had been a pride of Harlem.

It was at this low point in Wadleigh's history that the school joined a national nonprofit consortium, College for Every Student (CFES; n.d.). Over the first four years of the Wadleigh–CFES partnership, attendance showed a slight uptick, and a few more students attended college, but changes in school culture were extremely small (Newcomb & Michael, 2010). Then, in 2006, student performance and personal accountability increased dramatically throughout the school, eventually leading Wadleigh to an "A" rating—a rare accomplishment, given that the school six years earlier had been on the SUR (School Under Review) list (Newcomb & Michael, 2010).

What was responsible for this incredible change was that a team of Wadleigh students stepped up as leaders and transformed the school from "a gang culture to a college culture," says former principal Karen Watts. A group of seniors who called themselves Da Committee dreamed up and inaugurated the "100% Campaign," a student-led initiative whose goal was that every member of the senior class would attend college (Newcomb & Michael, 2010). Amazingly, every one of the 100 CFES scholars in the class of 2006 did attend college in the fall. To meet this lofty goal, student leaders supported each other through the college application process and mentored their younger peers, delivering a message that anything short of college was unacceptable.

"We changed our destiny and we had an impact on our classmates and lots of other kids," says Shameka Cobb, one of the student leaders in Wadleigh's class of 2006. What Shameka and her classmates accomplished exemplifies inclusive leadership. Inclusive leadership embodies the belief that all students are both capable of and have the responsibility to lead. They must play a role in making their schools and communities better places. To do so effectively, they must reach out to involve others, to inspire and encourage, becoming leaders in their own right (New York Life Foundation, 2007).

Wadleigh—now the Wadleigh Secondary School for the Performing and Visual Arts—is a perfect example of what can occur when the ingredients necessary for identifying and nurturing student leadership are present in school culture. In their case study, one can see the value of having adults (administrators, faculty, staff) who cared enough about their students that they were willing to invest in their leadership capacities; a group of students eager to step up to serve and lead; and external resources (training, professional support, and a national network of educators and students eager to share best practices and learn from one another) to augment those that the school provided. Students were encouraged, taught, and supported in becoming servant leaders, whose mission was both to improve their school and to build an inclusive school community that could carry on their work after they had graduated (New York Life Foundation, 2007).

THE CASE FOR INCLUSIVE LEADERSHIP

Wadleigh's success stands in direct contrast to national trends. While fewer American youth are stepping up to serve, this downward trend is amplified among underserved students—those from low-income households who would be the first in their families to attend college. Underserved youth are 50 percent less likely to participate in service activities than their more affluent peers. This is due in part to the unfortunate fact that they have fewer options for service. Even more disturbing is that these students are significantly less likely to take part in a school or youth club, which often provides opportunities for leadership experience (Spring, Dietz, & Grimm, 2006).

When students from low-income backgrounds take on leadership positions, however, they demonstrate the same level of commitment as their wealthier counterparts. Underserved students express a vested interest in volunteering to gain work experience, but the playing field is not level when it comes to their chances of becoming a student leader. It is schools' responsibility, therefore, to foster meaningful leadership opportunities for all young people, especially the underserved (Spring, Dietz, & Grimm, 2006).

National research shows the value and power of service (Ferlazzo, 2012; Spring, Dietz, & Grimm, 2006). Students involved with school-based service benefit in myriad ways. Among these are fulfilling an innate desire to help others; developing teamwork and the ability to work with diverse populations; and learning to respect others of different backgrounds, values, and opinions. Servant leadership increases students' self-confidence, leadership skills, and goal-setting and goal-achievement strategies (Ferlazzo, 2012). It also provides pathways to career identification and development (Spring, Dietz, & Grimm, 2006).

These attributes are what colleges and employers alike look for in emerging adults. Positive student outcomes resulting from leadership also will affect an entire school community as students show greater engagement in their studies, motivation to learn, respect for other students and teachers, increased attendance, and focused postsecondary aspirations (Ferlazzo, 2012; Spring, Dietz, & Grimm, 2006).

Leadership experience gives students early exposure to the world of work, allowing them to learn about different career and postsecondary paths. In turn, this can promote better choices when it comes time to select careers, academic majors, and colleges or advanced training after high school. Further, students report that taking part in service activities transforms their civic attitudes and behaviors. Underserved adolescents who have engaged in leadership through service are more likely to volunteer again in the future, more likely to discuss politics with friends and family, and more interested in current events (Spring, Dietz, & Grimm, 2006).

Giving back to others also influences psychological well-being. Being part of a leadership initiative fulfills many of Maslow's (1968) human needs. Students claim that leadership through service fosters in them a "more positive view of the future [and a stronger] belief not only in their personal ability to make a difference in solving community problems [but also in their sense that] people can be trusted" (Spring, Dietz, & Grimm, 2006, p. 32). They become skilled at locating and using resources, setting goals, managing their time, and thinking critically—skills and attitudes that boost students' resiliency on a college campus, particularly during the difficult transition from high school to freshman year of college. In fact, research shows that a crucial variable in a student's ability to persist and thrive in college is their involvement in at least one club, activity, or civic group (Tinto, 1993).

TRADITIONAL VIEWS OF LEADERSHIP

One of the major obstacles to inclusive leadership in schools is the very definition of *leadership* itself. Within schools and society in general, a formal definition of *leadership* holds sway, and those who attain such a status are expected to be well-respected, exercise sound judgment and authority, provide a vision for the institution, and determine policy and procedure. The belief remains that the achievement of such a level of authority is a reflection of a combination of experience, skills, and personality traits (Donaldson, 2007).

In the traditional view of leadership, only certain individuals possess the necessary inherent and professional characteristics that make them capable of being successful leaders (Donaldson, 2007). This hierarchical model of power and authority is believed to be necessary for the good of an institution, and it ensures that many stakeholders are excluded from power-sharing and leadership prospects by default.

Ambler (2013) combed through the work of those who write about leadership, looking at the many definitions of *leadership*, and identified a number of ways to conceptualize it. Among these are the traditional sense of leadership as influence and leadership as character (Donaldson, 2007). These qualities move closer to the concept of inclusive leadership, both in service and in the development of others. Adopting this perspective could remove the more restricted view of leadership that pervades most schools.

Countering a narrow vision of leadership requires seeking out, encouraging, and providing various supports for multiple leaders within a school community. This entails removing "structures of authority and control, which reproduce systemic inequalities in the wider society and run counter to democratic pedagogy" (Wallin, 2003, p. 63). It takes a bold school leader to do so, yet given the need for engaged stakeholders throughout the school and community, student leaders seem an obvious but often overlooked resource.

Part of the challenge is convincing students of the prodigious talents that they already possess.

HOW STUDENTS DEFINE *LEADER*

When asked to define *leader*, students often provide an exclusive—rather than inclusive—definition. Research conducted with 3,000 middle and high school students showed the same definitions repeatedly, leading to a narrow understanding of leadership roles and attributes that most students hold. The findings are grouped into two major categories: roles held and attitudes/actions (Michael & McKibben, 2006).

The results echo the early work of van Linden and Fertman, who distinguish between transactional and transformational student leadership. Most students would see leadership in the traditional, transactional mode, which is why they equate leadership with such actions as running meetings and telling others what to do (van Linden & Fertman, 1998). Transformational leadership, however, involves helping people to overcome their own self-interests for a larger good, and this is where leadership through service to others comes into play (Bush, 2011).

In the category of formal roles, students overwhelmingly mentioned leaders as captains of a sports team or those who lead a club, hold an elected office (such as student council), or belong to such a recognized organization as the National Honor Society. In terms of personal attributes and actions, leaders take charge of activities, are popular with other students, make decisions, don't hesitate to voice their opinions, and aren't afraid of speaking in front of groups (Michael & McKibben, 2006).

It is not shocking, then, that most students don't identify themselves as leaders. One problem in most contemporary schools is that there are only a few recognized leadership positions. Only a handful of students can be elected or chosen for formal positions, such as class president or team captain; often students are automatically excluded from these positions because of their grade point averages, inability to pay the dues, or other eligibility criteria (Michael & McKibben, 2006).

Underserved students are even more unlikely to view themselves as leaders. They may not see themselves as popular enough with enough students to be elected to leadership positions, and even if they were, many do not feel comfortable in the public spotlight because of culture, language barriers, or disabilities (Michael & McKibben, 2006). Many students fear that they may fail as a leader, while others are afraid that they may be alienated from their friends or peer groups because stepping into leadership roles is not desirable.

These answers reveal a variety of barriers—internal and external—that confront potential student leaders. Potential student leaders may let low self-esteem, lack of self-confidence, fear of responsibility or of carrying the burden alone, perceived lack of leadership skills, and shyness about speaking one's mind deter them from assuming leadership roles. These fears are often accompanied by concerns about losing friends, being unpopular, not being able to find enough time to lead, or making mistakes when one becomes a leader. In order to build leadership capacity among students, trusted adults and peer mentors can support these young people to transition into leadership roles (Michael & McKibben, 2006).

DEFINING *INCLUSIVE LEADERSHIP*

Unlike those adhering to traditional definitions of *leadership*, Ryan (2006) sees true leadership as a "collective influence process that promotes inclusion. Such leadership is inclusive in two ways" (p. 2). The two ways involve including as many individuals and groups and myriad values and perspectives as possible; doing so promotes inclusion, social justice, and democracy. Ryan notes that too many young students do not succeed in school because they are not included in ways that best promote their sense of community.

While all individuals are excluded at some time in their lives, certain student groups are excluded from full participation on a regular basis. If it is believed that only a few special individuals have the capacity to be leaders, then those who appear to be less capable or desirable as leaders will be systematically ignored and their leadership talents overlooked. Ryan (2006) stresses that "everyone deserves to be included fairly in all systems and practices of school and society" (p. 15).

Ryan does not argue that everyone should be included in the same way but that there should be fairness and equity. Inclusive student leadership entails presenting all students with the opportunity to develop as leaders and allowing each student to choose the form that fits best and has the most personal resonance (Ryan, 2006). Multiple definitions of *meaningful leadership* must be taught so that students can see an array of options for self-expression.

Ryan (2006) describes inclusive leadership practices as intentional and goal-driven. For schools to promote inclusive leadership, it is important that the end goal be defined in much the same way that Greenleaf (1977) did when he developed his theory of "servant leadership." In Greenleaf's definition, the only true leader is "seen as a servant first, and that simple fact is the key to his greatness" (p. 21).

Northouse (2012) points out that Greenleaf's definition asks leaders to have a "servant's heart." They are not servile yet want to help others by identifying and meeting their needs. The most fundamental characteristic of the servant leader is the desire to lead. There also are a number of other traits that make up the servant leader's character, such as the ability to listen to and validate others' perspectives, empathy and the ability to see others' point of view, healing, awareness of self and others, persuasive abilities, the ability to be a visionary, a knowledge of the past that permits foresight, stewardship, commitment to the growth of others, and the ability to build community.

National Urban Fellows (2018) was founded on the concept of inclusive leadership. They define *inclusive leadership* as one that "carefully includes the contributions of all stakeholders in the community or organization. Inclusion means being at the table at all levels of the organization, being a valued contributor and being fully responsible for your contribution to the ultimate result" (n.p.).

Inclusive leaders, according to Shambaugh (2017), share certain strategies, support a broad range of thinking perspectives, and are aware of their own biases or areas of comfort. Recognizing these areas allows true leaders to open up leadership possibilities for those who do not necessarily share their perspectives or who are not among their own close friends or inner circle of associates. They are open to alternative ways of viewing and solving problems, creating atmospheres of psychological safety so that divergent voices can be heard, and developing the capacities of others, and they are not afraid to share successes (Shambaugh, 2017).

A servant leader is one who serves others. When this concept of leadership is used as a school's definition, students can readily see the difference between leadership practiced by a small, select group of peers (usually very charismatic or forceful ones) who may influence others in ways or toward ends that are harmful, and authentic leaders who lead for the sole purpose of improving the lives of others, the community around them, and the global environment, as well as helping others to see their own innate leadership capacities (Shambaugh, 2017).

THE GOAL OF INCLUSIVE LEADERSHIP: SERVICE TO OTHERS

One of the greatest challenges of engaging all students in leadership roles and activities is making certain that all share in a common definition of *leading*. Developing a school culture of inclusive leadership begins with articulating a definition and using that definition in ensuing discussions about students as leaders (Shambaugh, 2017).

Leadership through service to others might best be defined, for the purpose of this chapter, as students taking action to improve or care for their school, local, state, national, or world communities. Student leaders work to bring out the best in others so that they can develop and strengthen their leadership capacities. Service leadership is action-oriented, with the end goal always being the improvement of the quality of life for others or the planet (Northouse, 2018).

Leadership through service is always positive in nature—bringing out the best in oneself and others (Greenleaf, 1998). This is an important concept to emphasize because examples abound of leaders who have misused their power, position, or charisma to influence others to act negatively or to abuse their status for personal gains. Leadership through service may find its expression in a venue as local as a first-grader's own classroom or as global as the adoption of a school in a faraway country.

Creating a school culture of student leadership engages young people of all income levels and abilities, breaking down barriers to participation and fostering a positive, inclusive learning environment (Shambaugh, 2017). As a result, there is a niche for all students as leaders, and all leadership styles can be valued and celebrated. Schools that engage all students articulate an expectation that leadership is something that everyone is involved in (Shambaugh, 2017).

Leadership skills must be identified, nurtured, and honed; therefore, there must be forums for developing student leadership skills through instruction and modeling. Leadership activities are important to postsecondary access; thus, students must be helped to recognize and document their leadership activities to support college and career pathways. Building a culture of leadership into a school's normal activities means that students who may not have the time or means to pursue out-of-school service opportunities can have these experiences within the school day (Spring, Dietz, & Grimm, 2006).

CREATING A CULTURE OF INCLUSIVE LEADERSHIP

Encouraging all students to envision themselves as leaders should be a school's mission; thus, schools must present and honor a variety of leadership styles. As part of their expressed mission, schools must publicize and act authentically on specific beliefs: leadership capacity is inherent in all students; there are myriad styles of leadership; leadership through service to others can be expressed at any age, developmental stage, or grade level; and leadership skills can be developed and refined through instruction and mentoring (Causton & Theoharis, 2014; Michael, 2006). Along with embracing an inclusive definition of *student leadership*, schools need to build a culture that supports leadership through service so that all students are able to see themselves as having a valued leadership service role in their schools or larger communities (Causton & Theoharis, 2014).

To help bring out the leader in every student, intentional instruction is needed for a range of important topics within the leadership umbrella:

- a clear definition of *inclusive leadership*
- multiple styles of leadership
- how to identify individual leadership styles and preferences
- research on the personal qualities of effective leaders and their skills
- how to identify assets and areas for additional training
- opportunities to be involved in all aspects of a service project—choosing the project, setting goals, developing a strategic plan, identifying resources, creating a timeline, articulating leadership roles, implementing the plan, and evaluating the success of the project (Michael, 2006)

Among the models for conceptualizing student leadership is one developed by Michael (2006) for the national nonprofit organization College for Every Student. In this model, students are introduced to the multiple ways of demonstrating leadership and encouraged to brainstorm new ways. Among the possible categories of leaders are mentors, tutors, coaches, environmentalists, and artists. Students also can demonstrate their leadership through scholarship, volunteering in the community, fund-raising, public speaking, or becoming trained as a peer mediator. They are invited to think of other ways that appeal to them, such as being an animal advocate or a global citizen who takes on a cause or project in conjunction with another country or culture.

HOW TO DEVELOP A SUCCESSFUL INCLUSIVE LEADERSHIP PROGRAM

In order to develop a quality program of inclusive leadership, schools are urged to consider the following steps in creating a plan that will fit their school communities (Causton & Theoharis, 2014; Robertson, 2016).

Identify the Purpose of the Program

For a leadership-through-service program to be successful, it must be tailored to the unique goals of each school, and each school must consider its own culture, diversity, geography, student profile, and community resources (Causton & Theoharis, 2014). Members of the school community must be clear about the rationale for focusing on leadership initiatives and buy into the goals of the program if they are to lend their support. Possible objectives for an inclusive leadership program might be to:

- improve school culture
- foster citizenships
- enhance parts of the curriculum
- build a greater sense of community within the school
- meet a graduation requirement
- promote college awareness and readiness
- raise global awareness through service
- extend existing service projects to new populations or age groups within the school
- develop partnerships with local organizations, including colleges or universities

Too often, schools launch into new projects for the right reasons but without taking the time to articulate the rationale for doing so and the objectives participants hope to achieve. When one begins a leadership program, engage stakeholders in a discussion of the purpose, plans, and desired outcomes. A discussion of the rationale for a leadership-through-service program should include the school mission and the program's inherent value for students. Questions to guide planning for inclusive leadership programs include the following:

- What definition of *leadership* would students at your school give if asked, "Who are the student leaders in your school?"
- Is the concept of leadership through service present in the academic curriculum in your school? If so, how? Where? Is there a service requirement for graduation?
- Do you have specific leadership-through-service goals for students? If so, are you on track to achieve those goals? Are there obstacles to achieving the goals? Are there resources that you need?
- Can you tap college partners for resources to support leadership-through-service training and activities? What about community and business partners? What specifically do you need from them? How will their involvement benefit their organizations?
- What criteria would you use to measure success in leadership-through-service activities?
- How would you involve students in tracking or archiving their involvement in leadership and service activities? Résumé, electronic portfolio, other?
- Are there students who demonstrate leadership outside of the school community? Are there ways to recognize their accomplishments within the school context, as well?
- What vehicles currently exist for soliciting student opinion about how leadership through service could best be encouraged, supported, and recognized in your school? (Causton & Theoharis, 2014)

Choose an Approach to Defining the Program

Just as there are many different reasons for launching a leadership-through-service program, there are many different approaches to consider:

- A learning-centered approach in which leadership-through-service projects are directly linked to curriculum. For example, students might learn about the environmental, social, and economic effects of pollution through a cleanup project.
- A service-centered approach in which leadership through service focuses on service for service's sake. An example would be giving back by holding dinners or social events for senior citizens.
- A community-building approach in which leadership-through-service activities are used to build or strengthen a sense of community and inclusion within the school. In this approach, older students might plan a transition

event for younger students to ease their movement from one grade to another.
- A school-culture approach in which key roles and responsibilities of the daily running of the school are taken on by student leaders. These students might conduct the morning announcements over the PA system or lead school assemblies. (Causton & Theoharis, 2014)

Build from Expertise That Already Exists

During the early stages of planning and implementing one's inclusive-leadership program, take stock of existing leadership training and service opportunities in your school and community. While some characteristics of a good leader are instinctive, many skills of effective leadership (setting goals, communicating, gathering data, managing diverse opinions) need to be modeled and taught. This is where resources of other partners can be an invaluable resource for aspiring student leaders. Contact other schools in your district; visit national leadership websites; check in with your college partners; or contact local, regional, or national organizations that promote student leadership and service to gather ideas. Ask others what has worked well and what they've learned from their mistakes. Questions to keep in mind when exploring existing initiatives include

- What forums for student leadership currently exist at your school? What's working well?
- What service activities are available through the school? Community? What has been successful?
- What leadership activities are recognized, celebrated, or rewarded at your school? Are there other kinds of leadership that you would like to recognize?
- What kinds of leadership training or education are offered in your school? Community? Are there skills that student leaders could benefit from that are not being taught? (Causton & Theoharis, 2014)

Borrow different aspects of other programs and learn from others' successes and challenges; however, in order to be a success, each school leadership program must be tailored to fit the culture, geography, student profile, and community resources of the school (Gavan, 2017).

Engage Students in the Entire Process

Aspects of high-impact leadership-through-service programs are the following:

- Scholars generate ideas for their service projects and by consensus choose those to implement.
- Scholars develop a step-by-step plan for the implementation of the project.
- Scholars delegate specific roles and responsibilities for those involved in the implementation of the project.
- Scholars develop a means of evaluation and opportunities to reflect on the success of the project.
- Scholars serve as spokespeople for presenting the project, disseminating crucial information, and reporting on and celebrating the success of the project.
- Each chosen leadership-through-service project is unique; it reflects the specific school and community in which it is set.
- There are opportunities for scholars to identify and develop leadership skills that they need to make the project successful.
- The project is developmentally appropriate for the age group involved.
- Whenever possible, each chosen project involves more than one of the CFES practices. (Causton & Theoharis, 2014; Griffiths, 2013)

Recruit Reluctant Leaders

It is impossible to overemphasize the importance of reaching out to students who have leadership potential but who might not see themselves as leaders. Even younger students, those in elementary and middle school, can be part of the planning process. In creating an effective leadership-through-service program, encourage all students to envision themselves as leaders capable of playing a valuable role in service to their schools or communities. Heath (2016) illustrates the importance of inclusion:

> A student body needs to be able to see leaders who look like them, who have the same interests and struggles as them, and who understand their unique strengths and basic needs. Schools that do not have a diverse student leadership sometimes unintentionally create situations that may alienate students instead of helping them feel included.
>
> Spirit Week is one example. A "Hawaiian," "redneck" or "nerd" dress up day has the potential to damage relationships. A pep assembly where male

football students wear female cheerleader outfits and negatively reinforce stereotypes has the potential to alienate instead of unite. If a more diverse group of students were involved in the planning of school events, then potential issues are more likely to [be] identified early and events that truly unite planned. (p. 23)

As you seek out potential leaders, consider these questions:

- What populations of students are most likely to be engaged in leadership-through-service activities at your school?
- What populations are least likely to be engaged? What are the barriers to their engagement? Who would be effective in recruiting them to engage in service activities and take on leadership roles? (Heath, 2016)

Develop Student Leadership Teams

The best way to develop student leaders is to give students leadership roles. While some schools use an application process to build its student leadership team, other schools use self-nomination or open membership. Whatever the strategy, membership should be inclusive, targeting obvious leaders as well as those whose leadership potential has yet to be tapped. Students should see all student leaders as having status and power to make meaningful changes in their schools. Let the student leaders select goals and activities that are important to them. If they are passionate about an activity or event, they will be motivated to follow through to completion (Causton & Theoharis, 2014; Griffiths, 2013).

While adults can be available to facilitate aspects of leadership-through-service activities, it is important that they leave the "nuts and bolts" of goal setting, short- and long-term planning, delegation of responsibilities, follow-up, implementation, and cleanup to the students themselves. Students should be invited to take part in meetings and other forums in which they, rather than the adults, make presentations, gather data, report on their findings, and make suggestions for planning activities (Heath, 2016).

Build a Cadre of Coaches

While most members of the student leadership team will be students, a high-functioning team will have a valued adult at the helm—someone who is well organized and not only comfortable relinquishing control but also able to recognize when student leaders are ready to take control (Griffiths, 2013).

These adults act as coaches. Rather than directing the projects, they may, among other functions, provide workshops on specific leadership skills, help scholars coordinate with community and college partners, and assist in reaching out to reluctant scholars who need to be invited into the projects. When possible, they also may work with other staff to incorporate leadership-through-service projects into the curriculum or service requirements of the school.

Collaborate with Key Stakeholders

As with student involvement, the earlier and more fully other key stakeholders are engaged in gathering information, brainstorming, and identifying resources, the more committed they will be to the program. Collaboration lightens the load for each partner and provides students with opportunities to make new connections and to work with others within and beyond the school community. During planning, consider inviting:

- local college partners
- community leaders and heads of local civic organizations
- leaders of area service organizations
- college or community mentors who serve in your school
- parent representatives

Among the many contributions that college and community partners can make are:

- hosting student leadership summits
- providing guest speakers for summits and other events
- holding leadership training sessions
- sending college students to mentor aspiring leaders at their schools
- generating ideas for service activities that would benefit the community
- inviting students to speak at their meetings
- working with high schools to offer credit-bearing leadership classes
- sponsoring service activities

Remember to solicit not only support for student leadership activities but also ideas for membership activities. A good leadership program should be a win-win proposition for all partners (Griffiths, 2013).

Promote, Publicize, and Celebrate Diverse Expressions of Student Leadership

Nothing motivates people to join a project like knowing that it is successful and that they will be recognized for their efforts, and while ultimately it is essential that students engage in service for its own sake, it is important to acknowledge their commitment and hard work. It is important that not just the obvious awards and recognitions—academic, athletic, and arts—are publicly celebrated, as too often only the most traditional forms of leadership have their ceremonies and awards banquets.

Once program goals have been set and planning has begun, student leaders should display these goals prominently in the school. Visual and oral articulations of leadership goals encourage students to stay on track and celebrate successful attainment of their goals (Causton & Theoharis, 2014; Griffiths, 2013).

An effective way of engaging students in an annual leadership role is to have a school-wide leadership challenge. Encourage students to declare their intentions of becoming leaders by posing this challenge: Publicize your service events through local news media and recognize those who have offered support. Students who wish to demonstrate service leadership through communications skills can post articles in the school newsletter, on the school website, or in local papers. Personal expressions of appreciation to community volunteers and contributors can be done through thank-you notes written by student leaders.

Integrate Leadership through Service with Other Practices and Activities

Leadership-through-service activities should not occur in a vacuum. Every individual in a school's community already is overwhelmed with expectations and responsibilities. No one has much free time to devote solely to one initiative. It is important, therefore, to look for opportunities to fuse leadership education with ongoing activities.

A school that values inclusive leadership integrates this practice in its curriculum rather than viewing service activities and leadership training as events that should occur outside of class time (Griffiths, 2013). Not only does this approach reinforce the fact that leadership comes in many different forms and expressions, but it also deals with a common and valid teacher concern—that is, with so many external mandates and expectations for classroom curriculum, where does one find the time for other worthwhile school initiatives? Examples of how leadership activities can be woven into the regular classroom curriculum are included here.

Social Studies, History, Global Studies, and Civics

- Who are some of the great leaders of history? Explain your choices.
- Have all of these individuals been positive leaders? Why or why not?
- Are there differences in cultural definitions of *leadership*?
- What are the leadership styles of leaders you admire?
- Has the same style of leadership been effective in different historical periods? Why or why not?
- What are examples of servant leaders throughout history? How have their contributions improved the world?
- What skills have world leaders demonstrated that have made them effective in their roles?
- What have been some of the most difficult leadership decisions throughout history? On what basis did leaders come to their decisions?
- What forms of government encourage citizens to become servant leaders?
- During what events have students taken leadership roles in influencing American or world politics?

English, Language Arts, and Journalism

- Read age-appropriate stories (fiction and nonfiction) about historical servant leaders. What qualities of leadership do you admire in these characters? What challenges did they face? What style of leadership did they exhibit? What strategies did they employ to address these challenges? What/who were their sources of inspiration, strength, and courage? What can you take away from these stories to apply to your own leadership?
- Write a letter to the editor on a subject that you feel strongly about. Why is this topic important? What suggestions do you have for addressing the problem? What type of leadership must be exhibited to address the problem successfully? How will society benefit by instituting the changes that you suggest?
- In your school or local newspaper or on your school website, start a "Leadership-through-Service Student of the Month," and honor students for service to the school, local, or global community. Interview students, and include information about the activities they are involved in, the

sources of their inspiration, the sorts of leadership skills they developed, and ways others can get involved.
- Choose an inspirational speech given by your favorite servant leader. Analyze the speech in terms of content, intent, audience, and techniques to persuade others to action. What were the outcomes of this speech in terms of action on a local, national, or global level?
- Use the inspirational speech as a model to develop and give your own speech on a topic that you feel should be addressed to improve your school, local, state, national, or global community. Consider your audience (classmates; teachers; school administration; local, state, national, or global leaders). What information must you present? What techniques could you use to persuade them to support your cause? What specific steps are you asking them to take? How will the group you are addressing benefit? How will you evaluate the effectiveness of your oral presentation?
- Write an original story in which one or more of the characters demonstrates leadership through service. Read the story with younger students in your school, and have them talk with you about leadership through service. Have the younger students illustrate your story. Help the students write their own stories about leadership through service, either individually or in groups. Display their stories in the classroom or school, or feature them in your school newspaper or website.
- Write letters to businesses, organizations, and civic groups, requesting donations of money, services, publicity, or goods to support a service project that you are doing. Follow up with articles that publicize their contributions and thank-you letters expressing your appreciation for their support.

Visual and Performing Arts

- How have the arts been used throughout history as a means of demonstrating leadership? Consider the medium used, the historical challenges being addressed, the audience, the effectiveness of the artistic intervention, and the outcomes of the artistic strategies employed.
- Choose one past or contemporary artist, and investigate how they used the arts as a vehicle for expressing leadership through service. What social change were they hoping to bring about? What medium did they use?

Whom were they trying to influence? How successful do you think they were in bringing about the intended change?
- Choose one service project at the school, local, national, or global level that you care deeply about. What artistic medium could you employ to express leadership in influencing others to become aware of and take action on this project? How would you raise awareness and inspire others by using the arts? How would you evaluate the effectiveness of your artistic leadership related to this project?
- How have different cultures throughout the world employed the arts in leadership through service? What are some of the most prominent art forms and symbols that have been utilized to inspire individuals and nations to action?
- Work with a group of younger students in your school to use an art form of their choice to express an issue that they care about and would like to inspire others to become involved in. With your target population's age and developmental stage in mind, help the students identify an issue of concern, choose a vehicle of artistic expression (short skit, play, poster, etc.), create a project, and present their creation to an audience.

Science, Environmental Studies, Nutrition, and Health

- How has the concept of leadership through service been demonstrated in the scientific community throughout history? Who are some of the leaders? What styles of leadership have they demonstrated? What challenges did they face? How did their scientific contributions better the lives of others?
- Who are the environmental leaders in history? What challenges did they face? What actions did they take, and what leadership styles did they employ? How have their contributions made the environment better?
- What are the scientific and environmental challenges facing your school, local, national, or global community? What do you believe are the causes of these challenges? How could leadership through scientific and environmental service address these challenges?
- Choose one environmental issue that you would like to address. Develop a strategic leadership plan to bring about change at the school or local level.
- Work with a group of younger students in your school to identify a project of their choice to better the environment. Work with them to develop a

strategic plan for a group, classroom, or grade-level project to address their concern.
- How could you use your leadership ability to promote healthier lifestyles in your school or community? What are the local challenges involving such lifestyle aspects as nutrition, physical activity, substance use and abuse, mental health, poverty, or bullying? How might you take steps as a leader to identify and address one of these issues?

Math and Technology

- How has leadership through service been demonstrated in the math and technology worlds throughout history? Who are some of the leaders? What challenges did they face? What leadership styles did they demonstrate? How did they use math and technology to address the pressing human and global problems of their day?
- How could knowledge of statistics be useful in leadership-through-service initiatives? What are the different kinds of statistical data that can be used to persuade others to support your cause? How could data be presented in different ways to illustrate your position?
- How have historical and current leaders employed technology in service of their causes? What are various communication skills that such leaders needed?
- How could current technology be used to present, support, or evaluate a service project that you want to implement? What are the artistic and ethical challenges in using technology to support leadership projects? How might you use math in your decision making and in project evaluation?

Physical Education, Outdoor Leadership, and Athletics

- How have sports leaders throughout history used their sports and the athletic arenas to raise awareness of and address societal and global issues through service?
- Choose one sports leader whom you admire. How did he or she use his or her leadership abilities to serve the community, nation, or world? What types of leadership did he or she display? What issue did he or she address? What were the challenges? What strategies did he or she implement? What were the results?

- How could you and your teammates use your sport as a vehicle for positive change?
- How could you demonstrate outdoor leadership to engage others in your school or community to address challenges in your environment or to improve the health and wellness of others?
- How could sports teams or outdoor clubs create challenges with others to generate awareness, raise funds, or collect items for a service project?
- How could outdoor activities and cooperative games be used to develop leadership skills?

Foreign Language, Cultural Studies, and Travel Study

- Use your foreign language skills to communicate with students in another culture or country. Set up a joint service project that is carried out in both places, and report to each other on your progress, challenges, and successes. Use technology to illustrate your projects and to set up ePals or other electronic communications.
- Set up a joint leadership summit with schools from other parts of the state or country. Create sessions that deal with common issues of leadership, such as skills development, leadership styles, and leadership challenges. Also include opportunities for students from each school to present on their unique service projects and leadership initiatives.
- Investigate student leadership groups in various parts of the country and in different countries. Contact different groups to glean ideas for your own initiatives, and share challenges and successes in your school and community. Join leadership groups within various local and national organizations, or run for office.
- Study prominent leaders, including student leaders, in other cultures. What is unique about their leadership challenges and strategies? What is similar to your own?

FINAL THOUGHTS

Traditional, narrow, hierarchical definitions of *leadership* leave too many of our nation's students on the sidelines. An inclusive approach to leadership, with *leadership* defined as taking actions to improve the school, local, national, or global community and helping others develop their own leadership capacities, can transform a school's culture into one in which every student is seen as a potential leader and everyone in the school community is expected to lead (Causton & Theoharis, 2014; Griffiths, 2013). Given that there are myriad ways to express positive leadership through serving others, schools must commit themselves to providing the exposure and training in inclusive-leadership skills.

The playing field is not level when it comes to opportunities for young people to volunteer or hold leadership roles. Underserved populations are underrepresented when it comes to these experiences, so one goal of the school community is to become the hub of leadership training and experiences. Taking the approach that every student can help others, the environment, or the global community builds a culture of servant leadership in which each person can find a niche. Having leadership-through-service experiences at an early age prepares students to succeed at the postsecondary level through better choices in career paths, greater sense of self-efficacy, and high emotional quotient (EQ) developed through working with others of diverse backgrounds.

There are many resources and best practices that can help a school start or enhance a student leadership culture. Given the tsunami of mandates and change initiatives that threatens to drown the nation's teachers and administrators, it is wise to integrate leadership development into already-successful activities and classroom curriculum. It also behooves us to remember that sharing the power with well-trained student leaders lightens the collective load.

Burchard (2006) summarizes the transformative potential of student leadership in simple and clear terms: "Leadership provides us with unique and powerful challenges to grow and contribute. Leadership makes us aim our efforts, give of ourselves, and create meaningful relationships and changes. . . . We can, in a very real and authentic way, leave a lasting legacy through leadership" (p. 4).

POINTS TO REMEMBER

- Schools function far more effectively when all members feel valued and are seen as potential leaders.
- Students must understand leadership to be rooted in actions that aim to better the world around them and enhance others' capacities and potentials.

- Underserved populations historically have been left out of student leadership and service activities; thus, schools must act to level the playing field.
- Multiple, diverse definitions of *leadership* should be used so that all students can see possibilities for expressing their own power and potential.
- School personnel and students are overwhelmed with mandates and requirements; thus, school-leadership initiatives must be integrated into activities, curriculum, and practices that already exist to the greatest degree possible.
- Leadership-through-service education begins with the youngest students and forms a foundation for self-exploration that engenders postsecondary success.
- Multiple forms of student leadership should be encouraged and must be celebrated publicly in the same ways that we do with athletics, academics, and the arts.
- Community members, colleges, and established leadership organizations can be powerful partners in supporting student-leadership initiatives.

Chapter Three

Mentoring for Maximum Involvement

Making Marginalized Students Mainstream

In schools in which all students are engaged, no one sits on the sidelines. All students are seen as active participants in the school community, potential leaders, and capable scholars, no matter their background, academic profile, or personality traits. One of the most transformative practices for this kind of full participation is mentoring, which can be expressed in many different forms. Schools may make use of myriad mentoring models, including peer mentoring, college student mentoring, e-mentoring, or community mentoring (Wood & Mayo-Wilson, 2012). Inherent in each model is the basic concept that the mentor will help to guide his or her mentee to reach full potential and that, in turn, the mentor will grow from the mentoring experience (DuBois & Karcher, 2013; Kouzes & Posner, 2014).

Belt (2015) reports on a major mentoring study that found many benefits of school-based mentoring: 64 percent of mentored students developed more positive attitudes toward school; 58 percent achieved higher grades in math, languages, and social studies; and 64 percent achieved higher levels of self-confidence. These findings were coupled with others: 46 percent were less likely to use drugs, 53 percent were less likely to be truant, and 27 percent were less likely to begin alcohol use. Mentoring's goals include improved social competence, strengthened attachment, and increased social capital through introducing students to new connections. Equally important, relationships with caring adults may build resilience, and having a mentor can reduce social isolation in school (Wood & Mayo-Wilson, 2012).

DuBois and Karcher note that there have been many recent developments in the field of mentoring. Among these are a more nuanced conceptualization of mentoring to include the components of activity, relationship, intervention, public policy, and societal views on and willingness to engage in mentoring (DuBois & Karcher, 2013; Kouzes & Posner, 2014). The heightened interest most likely is in response to the ostensible successes (although frequently without research having been done) of mentoring programs to address the growing needs of our youth population, both in and out of school.

HISTORICAL ROOTS OF MENTORING

An oft-cited story is that of Mentor from Homer's *The Odyssey* (1996). Odysseus, king of Ithaca, must go off to fight in the Trojan War and leaves the care of his household to Mentor, who serves as teacher and overseer of Odysseus's son, Telemachus. After the war ends, Odysseus is condemned to wander vainly for 10 years in his attempt to return home. During that time, the now fully grown Telemachus goes out to search for his father. Athena, goddess of war and patroness of the arts and industry, secretly takes on the form of Mentor and accompanies Telemachus on his journey. Eventually, father and son are reunited and cast out would-be usurpers of Odysseus's throne and Telemachus's birthright (Shea, 1997).

There is other evidence, however, of mentoring throughout history and among different cultures; for example, in ancient Africa, well before the time of the Greek and Roman invasions, each time that an infant was born, the village shared responsibility for raising the child and inculcating its specific knowledge, practices, and values. There always was one older child, not a family member, who was assigned the responsibility to ask questions and listen intently to the younger child (Howard, 2016).

As early as 12,000 to 9,000 BC, in a prehistoric cave in the Pyrenees in southern France, ceiling paintings depicted a common theme: A group of men takes children to what then was considered the end of the physical world. The men encourage the children to be brave and extend their reach beyond the horizons of the present world (Bradshaw Foundation, 2011). Some scholars believe that the word *mentor* is loosely derived from these "men" taking children "on a tour."

François Fénelon became the tutor to King Louis XIV's grandson in 1698. Through *Les Aventures de Télémaque*, the most popular book written in the eithteenth century, Fénelon provided instruction to the young boy.

Using the term *sage counselor* to describe the main character, Minerva, who appears as Mentor, the tutor guided his student in how to become a wise and peaceful king; this instructor's political views offended the king, who fired him from his tutorial position (Clarke, 1977).

Popular culture also is rife with mentor–mentee relationships. Oprah was mentored by Maya Angelou, Mark Zuckerberg by Steve Jobs, and Martin Luther King Jr. by Dr. Berry Mayes (Rhodes, 2015). Other prominent pairs include Yoda and Luke Skywalker, Professor Dumbledore and Harry Potter, and the Genie and Aladdin. Charlotte in *Charlotte's Web*, the animal mentors to Mowgli in *Jungle Book*, and the old stag in Salten's version of *Bambi*, all fill the true role of mentor, which transcends that of mere friend to embody the hierarchical nature of mentorship, where the mentor transmits the qualities of intellectual and moral virtue to the mentee (Guroian, 2008).

Regardless of actual origin, the word *mentor* evolved to mean trusted advisor, friend, teacher, and wise person. Mentoring relationships are found throughout history and are fundamental to human development, where one person invests time, energy, and personal knowledge in assisting the growth and talents of another person.

MENTORING FOR POSITIVE YOUTH DEVELOPMENT

Lerner, Napolitano, Boyd, Mueller, and Callina (2014) note a movement away from risk and deficit models when developing mentoring models. Instead, programs are seen as integral to healthy development, and mentoring resources are viewed as developmental assets; thus, the "link between positive youth development and people as developmental assets suggests that mentoring may be a key resource in the lives of youth. We define effective mentoring as sustained, high-quality, and skill-building relationships between youth and adults" (p. 17).

Positive youth development, according to the Lerner et al. (2014), is comprised of the five Cs: competence, confidence, connection, character, and caring or compassion; others have suggested a sixth C, contribution. A checklist exists to guide mentors in developing each of the Cs within their mentees (see Lerner et al., 2014).

Cavell and Elledge see mentoring as an extension of preventative science, whose goal is to reduce the likelihood of a child developing vulnerabilities or negative health conditions. Youth mentoring can be seen in terms of relationships or contexts: "Youth mentoring is the practice of using program-sponsored relationships between identified youth and older volunteers (or paraprofessionals) as a context for prevention-focused activities and experiences" (Cavell & Elledge, 2014, p. 37). These programs can be academic, personal, or career-oriented in nature and long-term or short-term, such as an academic mentoring program to bolster skills and knowledge so that a student does not fall behind.

NATURAL MENTORS

Among the different types of mentors are those called natural mentors, who are caring, supportive adults found naturally in students' extended social networks. They might be coaches; pastors; neighbors; community members; and such extended family as aunts, uncles, and grandparents. Natural mentors play prominent roles in cultures in which family is venerated or where trust and familiarities with those outside the culture are lacking or underdeveloped (Hurd & Sellers, 2013).

The quality and duration of the natural mentoring relationship has implications for student outcomes. Relationships that last longer (five years or more), meet frequently (two to five times each week), and demonstrate greater levels of closeness result in higher levels of social skills and academic engagement. Mentees who report only moderate levels of closeness with their mentors fare no better than those who have no natural mentors. The most effective mentor–mentee relationships are those with older mentors, those who are racially matched, and those that involve a natural mentor who was related to the mentee. Strong mentoring relationships feed into greater academic engagement and improve social skills and psychological well-being (Hurd & Sellers, 2013).

Schools can connect with parents and communities to promote the value of natural mentoring. Older adults may have the time and commitment to enter into long-term relationships with mentees, and neighborhoods and community organizations may be able to diversify mentoring partnerships, especially in schools in which there are high majority populations among the adults (Black, Grenard, Sussman, & Rohrbach, 2010).

Adolescents spend large amounts of their time at school and in afterschool programs, which have the potential to promote prosocial activities and pursuits (Wentzel, 2015). If they are not engaged in such activities, however, they are more likely to become involved in substance use and other problem behaviors. Adolescents' relationships with nonparental adults, particularly school personnel, can result in natural mentoring relationships that influence school engagement and deter risk behavior. These relationships encourage school attachment that is then associated with a reduction in risk behaviors, including violence, drug and alcohol use, and binge drinking (Black et al., 2010). These results are significant above and beyond the potential influence of age, gender, ethnicity, and household composition. School is a crucial venue in which various aspects of development beyond academic learning occur. Caring teachers and other adults at school can bolster socioemotional, cognitive, and identity development.

Black et al.'s (2010) findings have implications for formal mentoring programs. School-based mentoring programs can integrate mentors into the school structure in ways that encourage school attachment and reduce problem behaviors. Schools should be encouraged to consider individuals beyond the obvious personnel (teachers and coaches); many students have powerful relationships with cafeteria workers, custodians, and bus drivers, for example. These individuals can be trained to augment their job descriptions with mentoring roles based on professional training and celebrated with a variety of recognition and compensation.

The presence of natural mentors seems particularly important in the development of students of color. Rather than viewing black youth as at risk, Black et al. (2010) see them as having a multitude of resources in natural mentors. This is particularly true for black youth with "vigilant parents"— those who are responsive to their children's needs and emotions but who hold extremely high expectations for them, regardless of circumstance. Black youth, according to Hurd, Varner, and Rowley (2013), have higher percentages of natural mentors than their peers, and the majority of these are kin-based. Students with natural mentoring relationships have greater levels of involved vigilant parenting, with most relationships lasting longer than a year.

Mentoring may actually improve parental relationships, as well. Parents who go out of their way to seek, foster, and encourage natural mentoring relationships build the resource "bank" of supportive others who cared about their children's development; parents and natural mentors share the responsibility of students' prosocial development (Hurd et al., 2013). This finding may be particularly important for single-parent or other households, where time, energy, and resources for prosocial parenting may be diminished.

Cooper, Brown, Metzger, Clinton, and Guthrie (2012) point out that mentors can buffer racial discrimination for African American youth. For both male and female adolescents, racial discrimination in a variety of forms is associated with school suspensions and self-reported depressive symptoms. Protective factors derived from natural mentoring with girls moderates the association of discrimination and school suspensions. Boys have more positive psychological adjustment and fewer depressive symptoms with mentoring, but boys without mentors have more school behavioral problems and lower school engagement. Because natural mentoring has protective effects, school–family–community relationships are crucial to the development of wrap-around support for youth.

MODELS OF MENTORING

Teacher Mentoring

Teacher mentoring of students can have impact in ways that other models may not, given the teacher's proximity to students and knowledge of school culture. Further, students must identify favorably with teachers in order to be successful. In particular, teacher mentoring can help students think of themselves as classroom contributors and care about learning and cultivate a greater sense of educational self-efficacy (Simoes, 2014).

Teacher-mentor programs can use teachers as mentors for their own students or those who are a good match for a particular mentee in terms of personality, interests, academic need, or discipline. Lopez (2012) notes that the best teacher-mentors have such traits as the ability to relate to struggling students, flexibility, a caring attitude, and the ability to impart a joy of learning. They hold high expectations for their mentees, find ways to meet standards without dumbing down the curriculum, have good classroom management skills, and are able to build rapport with students and their families (Simoes, 2014).

Effective teacher-mentors are patient, good communicators, and consistent and follow through on their commitments to students; as such, they can engender trust and recognize that relational aspects of education are most crucial in student engagement. They respect each student's viewpoint and are able to keep relationships alive, even during difficult stages in which it appears that a student may not be involved. Teachers and other academic support staff can be vital in mentoring efforts, as they can observe aspects of students that may be missed by others, affirm a student's strengths and talents, and develop targeted interventions specific to each student's needs (Simoes, 2014).

There is no one model of teacher mentoring, as there are many factors that influence the individuals involved and their needs. One example of cross-classroom mentoring is a mentor program that pairs each participating teacher with a student from another classroom. By spending time with and listening to the student, the teacher-mentor is often able to discover how to best meet the child's needs (Martin, 2011). Martin describes how one second-grader was having trouble cooperating and playing with friends during lunch and recess. The boy's teacher suggested that his mentor meet up with the child during lunchtime. The mentor began eating lunch with him regularly in the cafeteria, which led to more self-confidence in the student and a better lunch experience.

Mentors may also play an important role by attending school functions when the child's family cannot be present. Martin notes the example of a third-grade student's class that had had several publishing parties that the child's parents could never attend because of work conflicts. The student's mentor made certain to stop in and talk with the student about her writing and acknowledge her progress.

The teacher-mentor usually devotes 10 to 15 minutes per week with the child before, after, or during school. This time can be spent together all at once or broken into segments. The pairs choose the time that works best for them and for the student's classroom teacher. Among common activities are getting snacks, playing a game, talking, playing basketball or a sport, doing an art or craft project, or reading from the student's independent reading book. Teacher-mentors have found that interviewing each other is a great ice breaker, and they use the interview as an opportunity to find out if the student has any special interests that they can pursue in future meetings (Martin, 2011).

Community Mentoring

Mentoring opportunities that take place in the community can provide exposure to work and career experiences, as well as familiarize students and their parents with the resources that a community has to offer. One in three young people in this country will reach adulthood without having had a mentor in their lives. This leaves 16 million youth between the ages of 8 and 18—including 9 million at-risk youth—without any form of mentoring relationship (Bruce & Bridgeland, 2014). In addition to filling this gap, starting a youth-mentoring program benefits a company and its employees by building business acumen, providing management and talent development experience to participating employees, and improving performance while getting out in the community and clearly demonstrating a business's civic engagement (Anderson, 2017).

There is a centuries-long tradition of strong societies nurturing the next generation of workers, craftsmen, and artists by using such relationships as apprenticeships, internships, and formal guilds to support youth in finding suitable, meaningful vocations. Through the intentional guiding and educating of youth to discover and train for rewarding careers, communities and even entire nations have helped to create a stable social foundation, the continuity of goods and services, and a new generation of citizens who can make contributions to the larger society. As such, Altobello and Shapiro (2017) point out

> The transition from childhood and adolescence to young adulthood and a career path has become far too perilous and unpredictable for many of the country's youth. In spite of our nation's considerable resources, too many of our youth are impacted by poverty and community violence, too many of our students struggle to complete their education, and too many young adults have trouble finding a career foothold in our current economy. Clearly, we must do more to nurture youth through their challenges, ensure their personal and educational development, and support their efforts to join and contribute to our workforce. (p. 3)

There are 5.6 million youth (ages 16 to 24) disconnected from education and work. One in five did not finish high school in 2013, and only 52 percent were employed during the summer of 2014. Increasing the national business community's involvement in youth mentoring will create a more engaged and better prepared student population, ready to enter the workforce in meaningful ways. Research on 18 companies engaged with corporate youth mentoring determined that there are four key reasons for their involvement, including fostering engagement among employees and students, cultivating the workforce of the future, supporting communities, and aligning corporate strengths with mentoring needs. The companies of the study believed that they needed to take responsibility for better preparing youth for the jobs of the future. It is estimated that more 60 percent of all new jobs in the next decade will require some postsecondary education, "yet far too many youth struggle to build the skills needed to enter college. They also often lack the financial resources and support networks required to make it to college graduation" (Altobello & Shapiro, 2017, p. 10).

There are a variety of community-mentoring models: direct mentoring in the schools, mentoring in schools through nonprofit partnerships, and mentoring programs that take place in businesses and corporations. A number of corporate programs, such as Bank of America's YearUP, focus more intentionally on older students who are about to head into career and postsecondary opportunities. Of the 18 organizations studied, all encouraged employees to be mentors and made it possible for them to volunteer during business hours; however, the mentoring models for business partnerships varied (Altobello & Shapiro, 2017).

Most of the programs connected mentors and mentees in person, yet a few used e-mentoring exclusively or in combination. Where employees travel frequently, e-mentoring works best. Many companies bring students to the workplace, believing that exposure to the work environment serves as motivation and makes it easier for workers to volunteer; however, transportation and time away from school may be complications (Altobello & Shapiro, 2017). Mentoring in schools allows for connections with key educational personnel on behalf of the mentee.

All of the business mentoring programs shared some goals with the general social and academic goals of all mentoring programs and placed heavy emphasis on persistence to graduation, career exploration, specific skill development for success in any workplace, and promotion of STEM topics or careers (Altobello & Shapiro, 2017). A step-by-step approach to creating a business mentoring program that provides a good fit for each company or organization is outlined by Anderson (2017):

Brainstorm What the Company Can Offer Youth

Think about what the business can contribute to the youth in your community. What knowledge can specific individuals share? If it is a financial business, for example, employees might coach young people on how to budget, save for college, or reconcile their accounts, while gym owners might offer fitness and nutrition classes to promote the health of local youth. Business owners might host regular youth-run book clubs, poetry readings, or art exhibits on the premises, with employees acting as guides and facilitators. The best ideas will draw on the employees' expertise and relate to the type of business owned.

Brainstorm Work Experiences for Youth

One thing that any small business can provide is work experience and the opportunity for young people to shadow owners and employers. Restaurant owners might have students learn to keep the books and track inventory, while others might work in the kitchen. Mentors can then become references that young people can use for job and scholarship applications.

Connect with Existing Local Programs

Once there is a vision for the program, it is important to understand community needs and volunteer opportunities. Youth-mentoring programs can be started from scratch if necessary; however, there are often existing programs to partner with. The Mentor Program, for example, has an affiliate network across the country, and local organizations can be sought out online.

Plan for the Mentoring Sessions

Start planning the activities that mentors and mentees will enjoy together, along with such important details as how often, how long, and where the mentoring sessions will take place. Items for thought include transportation, forms and permissions, and length of the partnership.

Implement Your Youth-Mentoring Program

Provide training for employees who choose to take advantage of this youth-mentoring opportunity. Ensure that everyone knows his or her role, level of commitment, goals, and the best practices of the program. Once everyone is on the same page, get started. It is also important to recognize and reward participating employees to motivate everyone to continue.

Group Mentoring

Kuperminc and Thomason mention that not a great deal of research has been conducted on group mentoring of P–12 students; however, groups have been used when there is a need for reaching more mentees, when the cost of mentoring programs is a factor, or when there are few resources for more individualized mentoring in a community. The authors write that, for some ethnic minority groups, as well, group mentoring is more culturally appropriate and desirable. It also is a better model for mentees whose orientation is more interdependent or who are uncomfortable in one-to-one settings (Kuperminc & Thomason, 2014).

Although group mentoring is not group therapy, there are many commonalities about what makes a group effective and what individuals can gain from the group experience. While research shows less relational intensity with mentors in group-mentoring formats, there are other benefits that are of equal value; among these are direct interactions with others in the group; peer identification and mutual support; the chance to observe how mentors relate with other mentees; and, in the case of comentored groups, the opportunity to see how individuals work together as a team (Kuperminc & Thomason, 2014).

Kuperminc and Thomason reveal that four to six is an ideal group membership and that cofacilitated groups work best. There are many social skills to be learned in a group; practicing these skills—such as empathy, support for others, group cohesion, and articulation—allows members to rehearse those skills that are transferable to other school situations. Developing group skills gives students confidence that can translate into social situations beyond the mentoring setting. Skilled group leaders, clear focus, and activities to build skills and social connections are needed for effective group mentoring (Kuperminc & Thomason, 2014).

Cross-Age Peer Mentoring

Karcher (2013) touts the value of cross-age peer mentoring, in which there are two or more years' difference in age between mentor and mentee; as an example, most programs employ middle or high school students with elementary mentees. This model has particular value for both parties involved; roles of responsibility benefit older students in their attitudes toward adults, their self-perceptions, and their engagement with school.

While Vygotsky's zone of proximal behavior demonstrates that individuals may grow intellectually when being stretched cognitively by someone slightly more advanced, Reissman's "helper therapy principle" suggests that the reverse can be true. The helper may grow in relation to the mentee through doing something worthwhile for others, "self-persuasion through persuading others," and feeling important through the recognized role of helper (Reissman, 1965, cited in Karcher, 2013, p. 236).

Karcher also references Kohut's (1977) self-psychology theory as useful in appreciating the power of cross-age peer mentoring. In the theory, Kohut stresses that "all humans seek from others opportunities to receive mirroring, to idolize other individuals, and to experience a sense of twinship or oneness with select others" (cited in Karcher, 2013, p. 237). A good mentor provides this for his or her mentee through empathy, praise, and attention; this process requires, though, that mentors be reliable, consistent, invested, and trustworthy.

Cross-age peer mentoring has been used to facilitate a sense of connection and belonging to school for students who may feel marginalized or different in some way (Karcher, 2013). Having a visible relationship with a valued older student provides social currency for the mentee. The mentor may also model appreciation for diversity to others at school, boosting a positive sense of identity in the mentee, as well as serving as a social connection, introducing mentees on the fringes to other individuals and groups.

A checklist for practitioners to help them consider aspects of successful programming, as well as offering purpose, training, monitoring, and assessment, are the foundational elements of any good program. Peer mentoring also works best when mentors have some sort of codified curriculum to guide them. This particular practice, done properly, has the double advantage of increasing prosocial behavior in both sets of participants. There is career value in the mentoring experience, especially for those drawn toward the helping professions and teaching, in that career-congruent skills can be developed and refined (Karcher, 2013).

E-Mentoring

With electronic media becoming an accepted and common means of communication, e-mentoring has become a possible way of addressing the need for more mentors. Shpigelman (2013) notes, "E-mentoring programs arose for many of the same reasons that FtF [face-to-face] mentoring programs were developed, that is, as a means to compensate when naturally occurring mentoring relationships were not equitably available" (p. 259). E-mentoring programs can be particularly important for creating educational and career opportunities for underrepresented populations, such as those in rural areas or in communities with limited resources.

Distance-mentoring technologies can include telementoring, online mentoring, or virtual mentoring. Most e-mentoring programs have been based on asynchronous communication, but there has been an expansion of programs to include telephone and video conferencing via the internet, as well as the use of webcams with instant-messaging systems (Shpigelman, 2013). As with other mentoring models, e-mentoring can occur with individual mentees or groups and can be based on different goals and tasks for the electronic exchanges.

Research points to a number of benefits and challenges to e-mentoring, which is essentially in its infancy as a model. As mentioned previously, it can be a tremendous boon for schools and communities that do not have lots of possible mentors or do not have college partners geographically close by to provide face-to-face opportunities. E-mentoring may attract different kinds of mentors who are drawn to the electronic relationship or may have transportation issues or less time to devote to overall mentoring. Using web forums to increase the visibility of e-mentoring relationships seems to motivate mentors and mentees to engage in and sustain their relationships (Shpigelman, 2013).

Mentees who were motivated to meet the e-mentoring program's goals and who had greater internet experience prior to entering the program were more likely to seek their mentor's guidance, to see the relationship as easy to maintain, and to believe that the technology is easy to use (Shpigelman, 2013). This implies that issues of computer literacy and intrinsic motivation need to be factored into e-mentoring prior to program launch. Other research suggests that e-mentoring is successful in helping at-risk youth achieve their goals of high school graduation and can fill a motivational gap when mentees do not have parental involvement in their education.

Some of the challenges of these programs still need to be worked out. These include overcoming the "digital divide," developing a greater social presence in e-mentoring relationships so that a mentee's emotions can be gauged accurately, solving technical glitches, building skills in language, and improving written expressive communications and reading comprehension (Shpigelman, 2013). E-mentoring may well be a wave of the future or may augment face-to-face activities, drawing in a new population of both mentors and mentees.

Postsecondary Partnerships

Colleges and universities also provide wonderful frameworks for mentoring programs due to their rich array of resources. Many academic majors require practicum and field experience, as well as possible service learning, and colleges promote mentoring among education, social work, criminal justice, and psychology students, in particular (Komosa-Hawkins, 2010). There are so many potential mentors within the college culture—from faculty or staff mentors, students, coaches, athletes, or clubs and organizations that wish to give back. The diversity on most campuses offers a natural cadre of mentors who match the background of P–12 students.

In order to interest higher-education institutions in forming partnerships, school mentoring initiatives must have clearly defined needs and rationales that fall within the institutions' purviews. Differences in scheduling of the institutions; transportation; and protocols for recruitment, screening, follow-up, and evaluation must be worked out. College students and personnel can serve multiple mentoring purposes simultaneously by supporting P–12 students, familiarizing them with campus culture, and demonstrating different career paths and their relationship to the curriculum that students are engaged in and can pursue once they matriculate (Komosa-Hawkins, 2010).

Creative Models to Fill the Mentoring Gap

Blad (2017) presents some interesting solutions to the gap in the number of students who need or want mentors and the number of mentors available nationwide. The Peer Group Connection program formed at Greene Central High School in North Carolina, for example, offers students class credit to guide younger students through the first-year experience, as ninth grade, nationally, is when many students exit school permanently. These peer mentors tend to be a better fit in the area of socioemotional skill development (Blad, 2017).

Another iteration allows students to recruit their own mentors from adults in their social environments. Mentoring can take place in group formats, designed by the students, or in one-to-one settings. Married couples may be recruited to be team mentors with students, and e-relationships based on shared interests allow far-flung professionals to mentor students in such wide-ranging topics as culture or STEM (Blad, 2017).

Adults who may not step up to mentor are hard-pressed to turn down a student who recruits them, and individuals who might not enter into a school-based mentoring relationship may be recruited to something, such as a transition program for youth in juvenile justice systems (Blad, 2017). Having students identify an adult they would like as a mentor may minimize the problem of awkward matching or motivation to be part of the program.

Another model involves matching students individually with adult mentors; the pairs then meet regularly to do activities with other mentoring pairs. This can ease anxiety surrounding mentoring or being mentored in a one-to-one setting (Blad, 2017).

PURPOSES FOR MENTORING

Mentoring for Developmental Assets

Probst argues that the true purpose of mentoring lies in helping to identify and nurture, as well as build new assets in mentees. Developmental assets help students grow up to be healthy adults who are engaged, productive citizens. The cumulative effect of developmental assets produces students who are less likely to engage in risky behaviors, thus increasing the likelihood of future successes (Probst, 2006).

Taking an assets-based approach rather than a "fix problems" approach to mentoring allows mentors to begin building relationships with their mentees from a stance of strength and positivity, which is more likely to be a foundation for a meaningful relationship (Probst, 2006). Seeing and helping mentees to see the assets each individual brings allows the relationship to start with what is working; once a trusting relationship is established, mentors can begin to address any deficits that impede the mentees' progress.

Probst (2006) notes two categories of developmental assets: external and internal. External assets include support, boundaries and expectations, constructive use of time, and empowerment. Support comes in the form of a web of people and places in which the mentee feels safe and valued. This entails collaboration among mentoring programs, schools, communities, and family members. The stronger the web, the greater a child's resilience. Boundaries and expectations must be clearly articulated in all mentoring programs, but again, the mentor models appropriate cultural norms and behaviors and rewards mentees for prosocial behavior.

Empowerment involves mentees feeling valued as individuals, being given opportunities to shine, and being equal contributors to setting goals for the mentoring relationship (Probst, 2006). A mentee can use time constructively to take part in creative activities, youth programs, service to others, community organizations, and positive time with family, as well as enjoying reading and self-directed learning.

Probst (2006) sees internal assets as comprised of commitment to learning, positive values, social competencies, and positive self-identity. Commitment to learning goes beyond doing well in school and encompasses all learning opportunities, formal and informal. Positive values define mentees and their interactions with others, so mentors can help them articulate what they value and learn how to manifest these values.

Social competencies include interpersonal and cultural competencies that permit individuals to interact well with others and make decisions in difficult situations. Positive identity also includes not only a feeling of self-worth but also a hopeful outlook on the future, a sense of purpose, and a confidence in having the skills necessary to achieve goals. Probst (2006) stresses the importance of parent and community engagement and training; however, participants will be more drawn to mentoring involvement when recruited through a strengths-based model.

Mentoring for Healing

Toxic stress during childhood is becoming far more prevalent. Events triggering such stress (e.g., abuse, neglect, loss, household mental illness, or household substance abuse) are on the uptick, and even though poverty is not normally considered as an adverse childhood experience, many would suggest that it is a form of trauma. Children who undergo adverse childhood experiences most often experience impairment, particularly in the emotional, behavioral, attachment, and cognitive domains (McCoy, 2017). School personnel are forced to take on more and more of these children's problems, which have ramifications for the classroom and school community; however, they are being stretched beyond their limits to address all needs. This has resulted in most resorting to multitiered support systems within their buildings and beyond (Rosen, 2018). Mentoring can be one of these tiers.

Healing from trauma can take place in many settings beyond the therapist's office, and mentoring venues are such places; further, the thrust of many mentoring programs is toward preventative measures that buffer against trauma and its outcomes (McCoy, 2017). Mentors can confirm a mentee's abilities and talents and teach mentees about threatening situations. They can also reaffirm safe adults as "alternative[s] to the automatic belief that all connections are unsafe. Mentors can provide a connection to rewire automatic reactions to more positive emotional responses" (McCoy, 2017, p. 14).

Mentoring Students Who Are at Risk

As early as the 1970s, mentoring was in the limelight as a possible remedy for the dismal educational and career prospects for underserved youth. Early focus was placed on business mentorship after studies that showed that those who had mentors were more likely to be financially successful at a younger age, be better educated, and have greater job and career satisfaction. This focus shifted to educational settings in the 1980s, with such programs as I Have a Dream, in which multimillionaire Eugene Lange promised a free college education to East Harlem sixth-graders if they graduated high school; this offer ignited mentoring movements aimed at combatting high dropout rates and promoting college attendance (Bashi, 1991).

Mentoring has the potential to turn at-risk students into those "at promise" to succeed. Lopez (2012) defines *at-risk students* as those who feel alienated from school, administrators, classmates, and teachers. They share some common characteristics: They are more likely to come from single-parent households, be home alone more than three hours per day, be at higher risk for pregnancy and drug use, and be unlikely to succeed in traditional school settings. Other variables of risk include low economic status, not having English as one's primary language, having a disability, being identified as a special education student, having moved frequently, possessing poor reading skills, undergoing multiple suspensions and expulsions, and being retained one or more years. No group is in greater need of mentoring than these students—those who have disabling cultural or medical conditions, are denied or have minimum equal opportunities and resources, and are in jeopardy of failing to become successful and meaningful members of society (Simoes, 2014).

Approximately one-third of all students in the United States are considered at risk for academic failure, yet before academic needs can be met, students must have their social and emotional needs addressed (Simoes, 2014). As self-esteem and self-confidence grow, at-risk students can then turn their energies to academic goals. According to Lopez (2012), schools have increasingly become a vital refuge for so many children and adolescents.

Good schools can be a protective shield to buffer fragile populations from the exigencies of life outside school walls (Bashi, 1991). Traditional schools in isolation cannot possibly deal with all the societal problems that may tax the health and well-being of at-risk students, as these include such huge issues as poverty, violence, abuse, and cultural assimilation. Mentoring can be seen as one tool in closing the achievement gap, engaging marginalized students, providing social and emotional support, and including students in the Success for All Foundation (2015).

This is an urgent task, Lopez (2012) notes, as the path to becoming a school dropout can begin as early as kindergarten. Students who drop out of high school were frequently held back between fifth and sixth grade, and many will exit the school system between eighth and ninth grade—particularly boys of color (Simoes, 2014). The younger the student is labeled at-risk, the higher the likelihood that he or she will experience a persistence of problem behaviors.

Mentoring New Refugee and Immigrant Populations

Among the most marginalized populations in contemporary American schools are students who are refugees or new immigrants. Such students face new schools, as well as language, cultural, dietary, and educational challenges, as they attempt to assimilate into a new country. Mentoring within schools and communities can provide a welcoming relationship that eases this transition and speeds social and educational integration (Oberoi, 2016).

Oberoi (2016) examined research on mentoring first-generation immigrant and refugee youth and found that both formal and informal mentoring relationships were beneficial in acculturation and social integration into one's new country, as well as promoting school and academic integration. Mentors may "act as cultural and system translators and interpreters." School-based mentoring programs must specifically address the needs of these populations and in doing so promote academic success, social integration, and acculturation through positive relationships with teachers, school personnel, and peers (Oberoi, 2016).

Other potentials of mentoring include promoting positive ethnic identity and a sense of school belonging, cross-cultural exchange and knowledge for all students, and family support in developing programs that connect new immigrant and refugee parents with the school and community resources. Rotich (2011) remarks that immigrant and refugee children and youth under the age of 18 are the fastest-growing segment of our population. But it is clear that, unless they receive appropriate interventions, "they will continue to face the possibility of being undereducated, underemployed, and underprepared to participate fully in society" (Rotich, 2011, p. 3).

Such programs as Faces around Us in urban North Carolina were initiated to provide mentoring to underserved immigrant and refugee children (Rotich, 2011). Its primary goal is to help students develop "resiliency against societal barriers and to help them experience equal success while integrating into the American culture and schools in general" (Rotich, 2011, p. 4). Mentors from local community colleges and private and public colleges and universities nearby were recruited, trained, and provided with support to work with small numbers of mentees. Evaluations revealed that there were positive benefits for both mentors and mentees, with the college students' interest in working with diverse youth stimulated. The program, like other successful programs to mentor this population, involved acculturation training, mentoring and tutoring, enrichment and recreational activities in the community and at school, and engagement of parents in their children's academic plan. Activities bolstered academic skills and were developed to allow the "youth to experience, believe and to understand their strengths and their potentialities" (Rotich, 2011, p. 5).

Such programs as Jump Start at the University of Maryland (2018) take mentoring a step further with a program that connects refugee youth in Baltimore with a series of programs designed to increase college access and success. In its program, college students are paired with 11th- and 12th-grade students in a "near-peer" college-mentoring experience that familiarizes them with college exploration, application, and preparation (University of Maryland, 2018).

Mentoring for Resilience

Rhodes (2002) presents theory and research on how mentoring builds resiliency in mentees and finds that the most significant relationships are those of adult mentors. Classic resiliency studies, such as those conducted by Garmezy and Rutter (1983), also found that the presence of even one natural mentor could be a buffering factor against stressors as serious as war. In their classic 30-year study of children from the island of Kauai, Werner and Smith (1992) found that, not only were children who thrived the ones who had natural mentors, but also they sought out mentors themselves and benefited from at least one consistent relationship over time. Sheehy (1986) calls these individuals "polestars."

In totality, myriad studies (Oberoi, 2016; Rhodes, 2002; Sheehy, 1986; Werner & Smith, 1992) uncovered consistent characteristics of resilient youth: resourcefulness, social ease and savviness, curiosity, compassion, the ability to conceptualize, and self-direction. Youth saw change as possible and rewarding, had ideals that were bigger than the self, used humor to cope, had healthy expectations and flexibility, were creative, held values, initiated relationships, and exercised self-discipline. They relied on intuition and had good insights about others, as well as healthy self-esteem and an internal locus of control. It is easy to understand how effective mentoring can bolster resiliency when mentors identify and support youth assets and mentees have viable models and advocates.

Mentoring for School Behavior and Connectedness

Gordon, Downey, and Bangert (2013) explored the effects of school-based mentoring on students' school behavior and connectedness. The research on 6th- to 10th-grade students was confined to mentoring that had the four prominent characteristics of school-based mentoring programs: school personnel referrals of mentees, adult mentors who meet weekly with mentees, mentoring sessions held on school grounds during the school day, and a combination of social and academic activities during mentoring time. Compared to control groups, students involved in school-based mentoring were found to have had significantly fewer absences and discipline referrals and reported significantly higher scores on four measures of connectedness. First-year mentees reported significantly higher scores on one measure of connectedness, which indicates that they were able to begin their experience with a greater sense of engagement (Gordon et al., 2013). This is an especially important finding, given the high levels of developmental, academic, and social challenges that contemporary middle school students encounter when they leave elementary school.

The study's definition of *connectedness* involved outward expressions of positive feelings and help-seeking behaviors. It is "not dependent on an internal personality trait, but is something that can be changed, improved, nurtured" (Gordon et al., 2013, p. 243). This is a hopeful aspect of mentoring, in that strong relationships between mentors and mentees build self-esteem through relationships that value and celebrate each child. Students in the mentoring group had stronger future orientations, suggesting a stronger sense of purpose and ambition, than those of control group members.

Schwartz, Rhodes, Chan, and Herrera (2011) report that not all students are equally suited for mentoring, as there is no substitute for "professional treatment for youths with serious emotional, behavioral, or academic problems, nor a necessary inoculation for all" (p. 451). Students' relational histories are important to consider in designing mentoring interventions; those who have a baseline of satisfactory yet not particularly strong relationships before beginning mentoring have more positive outcomes than those students with strongly positive or negative relationships (Schwartz et al., 2011).

Younger students are more likely to report better friendships and more disclosure to adult mentors than are adolescents; this may be the developmental function of adolescents' push for greater autonomy and the higher salience of peer interactions and romantic attachments (Schwartz et al., 2011). Beginning mentoring programs at earlier ages may help in relational development. Relationally strong students might reach the ceiling of what mentoring can provide, but they may be considered for mentor roles in peer-mentoring programs.

Students with very weak relational profiles most likely will need a concerted effort between both mental health providers and mentors to reap full benefits from mentoring programs (Schwartz et al., 2011). They also will need well-trained, committed adults who will stay the course in order to reverse earlier patterns of poor attachment. Rhodes (2002) is convinced that a poor or disrupted mentoring match is far worse than never having a mentor at all.

Mentoring for College Preparation

The undermatching phenomenon takes place when high-performing and highly qualified students choose relatively nonselective postsecondary institutions. This phenomenon is far more likely to take place among first-generation, low-income, and other marginalized and underserved students. Without family members, for the most part, who have graduated from college to encourage them, these students lack social networks and contact with potential adults who can help them maximize their postsecondary and career potential (Woods & Preciado, 2016).

Beyond academic achievement in P–12, successful college applicants need to have mastered the intricacies of the preparation, application, and financial aid processes. Those of lower socioeconomic status have fewer opportunities to engage in test preparation courses, coaching, or campus visits. Many schools use mentoring programs to bolster the chances of all students being able to attain their highest postsecondary aspirations. By raising the beliefs that they can and will succeed in college, mentors increase their mentees' capacity for high academic achievement. They also serve as role models and dispensers of "college knowledge" that may go missing in many households (Woods & Preciado, 2016).

There are mentoring benefits for both high and low academic-achieving students. For high achievers, mentors can prevent the undermatching phenomenon by helping students conduct realistic college searches based on their talents and interests; they also can suggest ways to finance education that students may think is out of their reach. For lower achievers, mentors can build skills in all domains and spark college interest through demonstrating the relationship of postsecondary education to students' dreams (Woods & Preciado, 2016). Mentors can model self-advocacy skills and make students aware of support services on campus, as well as connect them with summer and "bridge" programs prior to matriculation.

Certain characteristics of the mentor–mentee college connection are most salient. High-quality mentor–mentee relationships result in greater increases in student motivation, self-efficacy, and social norms related to college. Mentees' belief that their mentors are invested in their success significantly increases their positive attitudes about college, and students with the lowest baseline SAT scores show a strong correlation between their feeling that their mentor cares about their success and their positive responses to college (Woods & Preciado, 2016).

Mentoring to Support Diversity Education and Tolerance

There is a dearth of scholarly literature on the children of immigrant families and even less on the role that mentoring interventions might play in their acculturation, so Liao and Sanchez studied the role of mentors in the acculturation process of older Latino and Latina mentees as they began the transition to adulthood. Among their major findings is that cross-race mentors decrease perceived racism. Liao and Sanchez divided their participants into two groups: those with all same-race mentors and those with at least one cross-race mentor. Perceived discrimination was significant in the model, but those with at least one cross-race mentor had lower levels of perceived discrimination and higher levels of respect (Liao & Sanchez, 2015).

Having cross-race mentors may influence young people to interpret cross-race interactions differently and with less racism (Liao & Sanchez, 2015). More frequent contact with their mentors was seen in both the bicultural and marginalized acculturation groups; young people who had assimilated into the mainstream culture had less contact. Those trying to figure out their cultural status appeared to have greater need for contact with their mentors as they tried to sort out their identities in terms of society and community.

CREATING A QUALITY SCHOOL-BASED MENTORING PROGRAM

The first step in creating a school-based program (or any mentoring program, for that matter) is to articulate the goals of the program. There are many different kinds of goals, including social inclusion, academic achievement, special populations, college preparation, career preparation, literacy improvement, or social skills. The essential aspect is to be able to write the program goals clearly, succinctly, and in measurable terms. Means and times for evaluation are important details (Jucovy & Garringer, 2008).

Next, the size, scope, and location of the program must be determined. As always, it's better to start small and be successful than to overreach and fail. A timeline for development, implementation, and revision of the various steps of the process (publicizing, recruiting, screening, and training and matching mentors) must be established. Approval from administration and from the site need to be obtained (Jucovy & Garringer, 2008).

The building of a leadership team comes after. Its composition is determined, in large part, by the mentoring model chosen. The team will have primary responsibility for the daily operations of the program; however, there needs to be at least one point person or visible liaison. Whenever possible, it is valuable to have students engaged in the leadership team or, at the very least, have a student leadership subcommittee to give input on events and protocols (Jucovy & Garringer, 2008).

Securing buy-in from key constituents is essential to success. Having a clear rationale for the program is particularly important; in considering how overwhelmed with mandates and new initiatives most teachers are, it is crucial to think about how mentoring might dovetail with already-existing activities (Jucovy & Garringer, 2008). Having students pitch the idea may also make it more enticing.

Consideration of legal, financial, and logistical details falls to the appropriate adult team members, but students can be instrumental in thinking through such ideas as events, activities, publicity, and recruitment, as well as celebrations and publicity about the program (Jucovy & Garringer, 2008). It's best to have some sort of kickoff event or offer information to parents and family members at a well-attended activity, such as a school-opening gathering, concert, or sports event. Jucovy and Garringer suggest having a pilot year to test out and refine the program before large-scale recruitment.

Mentoring to Develop Goal Setting

One of the most valuable aspects of a quality mentoring relationship is that it can be used as a platform for developing goal-setting skills and goal pursuit. Balcazar and Keys (2014) stress that mentors should be specifically trained in goal setting prior to working with their mentees so that they have the knowledge and confidence to help mentees set and achieve their goals. They must establish a genuine relationship and rapport with their mentees so that they will trust the mentors and share meaningful goals. If goals are not valued by the mentees, there essentially is no purpose in goal-setting activities and pursuit.

It is most logical to integrate goal setting into mentoring programs that are future oriented and aim to help mentees become more self-directed. The mentee must be ready and willing to discuss his or her goals with the mentor, and the mentor must be reliable enough to remain in the goal-setting pursuit until the goal is achieved or mutually renegotiated. The team must work together to set clearly articulated, achievable, and measurable goals. At times, larger goals will need to be broken down into more manageable, smaller goals (Balcazar & Keys, 2014).

The end result of all goal-setting-oriented mentoring should be to help mentees become more adept and independent in setting, tracking, and evaluating their goals (Jucovy & Garringer, 2008). While mentors can provide direct instruction in goal setting, they should let mentees take the lead in formulating the goals while taking into consideration their needs, interests, and desires. Additionally, goals should be consistent with each mentee's values and culture. Mentees should learn how to monitor their progress and adjust goals as necessary because this occurs in real life. All goal attainment should be celebrated (Balcazar & Keys, 2014).

The beauty of building goal-setting activities into mentoring relationships is that they can be adapted to any types of goals mentees have: social, academic, athletic, health and wellness, or behavioral (Jucovy & Garringer, 2008). These skills have a high degree of transferability to other venues and permit mentors to model how to get back on track if one's goal gets derailed. In a trusting mentoring relationship, mentors and mentees can share in formulating larger dream goals and see how to break those into attainable steps. They also can discuss ways to celebrate goal attainment in order to build greater growth toward intrinsic rewards.

Mentoring Students with Disabilities

Students with disabilities often find themselves socially marginalized and targets of discrimination, bullying, or isolation in contemporary schools. Having a mentor or being part of a mentoring program can create social capital and buffer such students from loneliness and depression. Young people with disabilities encounter challenges when attempting to access postsecondary options, such as higher education or the labor market. They are less likely to go to college or to be employed than are their peers without disabilities. A meta-analysis of studies on mentoring interventions for youth with disabilities discovered that there were many types of mentoring models aimed at increasing the likelihood of college or career success (Lindsay, Hartman, & Fellin, 2016). Among these models are school-based, community-based, job site–based, online, and multicomponent models.

Quality mentoring programs for youth with disabilities share some common features. First, they are longer in duration (six months or more), allowing relationships to truly develop. They have structure and often a codified curriculum. These successful programs employ paid mentor coordinators, and training is provided to anyone who serves in a mentor's role. Finally, there is continuous oversight of the program (Lindsay et al., 2016).

There is an interesting variable when considering mentoring programs for youth with disabilities: whether the mentor also has a disability. Students with disabilities with mentors who share that characteristic develop more knowledge of strategies to overcoming challenges to their independence (Britner et al., 2006). Children who are deaf and have mentors who are also deaf have increased communications skills, and their families gain a deeper appreciation of deaf culture.

Teaching self-efficacy skills to students with learning disabilities (LD) has an additional payoff for students. In a curriculum designed to help these students recruit their own mentors, set goals, and develop action plans, students who successfully completed the program and found mentors met a significantly larger number of their goals than those in the comparison group (Britner et al., 2006).

Students who are academically at risk tend to fare better in community- or work setting–based mentoring programs than in school-based models; however, reasons for this difference are not necessarily clear. Students who are at risk do perform better in school settings in such areas as reducing aggression and increasing attendance, prosocial behavior, vocational skills, participation in college preparatory activities, and postsecondary educational attainment.

The most effective mentoring relationships are secure and stable and last over time (Britner et al., 2006).

Mentoring is perhaps one of the most powerful socioemotional tools in preparing for the transition to college—for students with or without learning disabilities. Matching secondary students with learning disabilities with older, more experienced students who share their disability and yet have found success on the college campus is particularly effective because it is more likely that students with learning disabilities will listen to a mentor who has shared experiences (Britner et al., 2006). The mentor can answer questions honestly, provide strategies that worked for him or her, simulate situations that might be encountered on campus, help the secondary student rehearse for those scenarios, and assist the student in developing networks and relationships prior to actual arrival on campus.

Most colleges and universities can help high schools set up such mentoring programs through their office of disabilities services; larger institutions have designated mentoring personnel who run a variety of different kinds of mentoring: academic, sports, service organizations, and affinity groups. Schools also can set up mentoring experiences, in person or through e-mentoring, with their own alumni who have learning disabilities and have been successful.

Nationwide, there are mentoring programs specifically targeting students with learning disabilities. Eye to Eye's (2018) mission statement reads,

> Research on risk and resilience suggests that the most important factors that determine success for adults with LD/ADHD is not IQ or academic success, but self-esteem, self-awareness, and self-determination. Our fundamental mission is to give hope to younger students with LD/ADHD by introducing them to mentors with similar labels who can demonstrate the power and importance of goal-setting, securing individualized accommodations, and self-advocacy skills. (n.p.)

The program centers on techniques that mentors teach mentees, such as metacognitive skills, self-advocacy, and proactive learning strategies. Additionally, "they showed positive integration of learning differences and their LD/ADHD label into their identities. . . . [R]esearch has consistently demonstrated that these skills are fundamental to the successful transition of youth with learning disabilities into higher education" (Eye to Eye, 2018).

Gender Considerations

Liang, Bogat, and Duffy (2013) reviewed the studies on gender and mentoring that have been conducted and highlight some differences between genders that have implications for mentoring programs. Boys may need to be recruited on the basis of group activities, as they prefer mentoring that centers on being active and that involves other peers. Boys tend to be socialized away from help-seeking behaviors; if they seek help, it is more apt to be from friends, especially as they grow older, which is why mentoring groups based around forming "brotherhoods" may work best for them (Liang et al., 2013).

Girls seem to be more open to mentoring because of the high value they place on intimacy and connection; they are also more apt to seek help when under stress or emotional conflict. Girls take longer to form trusting bonds with mentors and are more vulnerable to negative effects if a mentoring relationship goes astray (Liang et al., 2013). As they move into adolescence and consolidate identity formation, it is important for them (and other marginalized groups) to be able to relate to strong, accomplished mentors of their own gender.

Same-gender mentoring is most often employed, especially as students grow older, to avoid any hint of sexual inappropriateness if a mentor takes an interest in his or her mentee (Liang et al., 2013). Formal mentoring that is long term seems particularly beneficial to girls, especially those with attachment issues that prevent mentoring from natural mentors.

CHARACTERISTICS OF A QUALITY MENTORING PROGRAM

High-quality mentoring programs come in all shapes and sizes, but they share some common characteristics. Among these are clear and well-understood goals, professional training for mentors, continuous oversight, regular evaluation, good matches between mentors and mentees, positive publicity, commitment, and celebration of successes (Eye to Eye, 2018). Using evidence-based guidelines for creating programs, business-based models share these characteristics. Recruitment of the right employees to become mentors is essential. As with all mentoring programs, potential mentors must be properly vetted and screened. Though mentors may have well-honed knowledge of their craft, they may need specific training on how to become an effective mentor (Altobello & Shapiro, 2017).

Another issue is matching mentor and mentee, and the best programs are very intentional in how they make their matches. Continuous check-ins permit both mentor and mentee to express how the relationship is progressing, allow for problem solving, and provide resources that support the match. An oft-forgotten aspect of mentoring is closure; good programs provide closure opportunities and celebrations of the relationship prior to termination (Altobello & Shapiro, 2017).

BEST PRACTICES FOR SCHOOL-BASED MENTORING PROGRAMS

Those programs that are most successful share some characteristics. The first is that mentoring is relational, so that the quality of relationship between student and mentor is essential. Making good matches and providing structures that build relationships leads to higher academic and connection outcomes. Facilitating interpersonal engagement appears to influence other factors. Older mentors seem to be more successful, longer-term relationships generally are more effective, and mentor training is important. Students prefer programs that have a mix of fun and games and relational activities.

Komosa-Hawkins (2010) warns that developing a stellar mentoring program is a complex process, with most of the work in the planning stage. Program developers must collect input from all stakeholders and listen to their voices in order to build buy-in and tailor the program to specified needs. School counselors, she mentions, are invaluable in the planning process, as they understand scheduling and unmet needs and have ready access to students. The best programs are grounded in theory and meet specific standards and benchmarks (Garringer et al., 2015).

It is rare to have volunteer mentors commit beyond one year; therefore, schools must think about turnover and recruitment, as well as closure protocols. It is easier to recruit and retain mentors if they are recognized and celebrated for their contributions and if programs can demonstrate, through rigorous evaluation procedures, that they are making a difference.

FINAL THOUGHTS

Rhodes (2002) makes a compelling case for the value of quality mentoring and the need for school-based programs in the battle against disengaged and disoriented students of all ages. Those school mentoring programs that can engage such additional partners as colleges, community members, and family stand a far better chance of reaching students whose true potentials lie untapped.

In its best form, mentoring is a multipronged tool to promote valuable outcomes. Among these are school engagement, motivation to graduate, interest in postsecondary education, civic involvement, personal health and well-being, acceptance of diversity, and academic achievement. Having a meaningful mentoring relationship reduces the chances of isolation and disengagement and bolsters personal resilience and self-efficacy.

In building solid mentoring programs, schools also can equip family members to be valuable partners in their children's education, as well as introducing them to resources within the school and community. Mentors who are "caring, capable, and committed adults" and invested in the lives of young people are "one of the most important contributors to positive youth development. Simply put, mentors matter" (Altobello & Shapiro, 2017, p. 7).

POINTS TO REMEMBER

- Mentoring can provide a sense of connection to the larger school community and is thus especially important for marginalized or disengaged students.
- There are many effective models of mentoring, which include peer, teacher, community, college, and e-mentoring relationships.
- Mentoring programs can be used to improve academics, social skills, career preparation, student engagement, or college knowledge and readiness.
- All quality mentoring programs share some similar characteristics, including a clear statement of purpose, consideration of school and community resources, regular contact between mentor and mentee, goal setting, a combination of purposeful and fun activities, frequent check-ins, celebration and recognition, and ongoing assessment of program success.
- Schools can work with parents and extended family members, who often serve as "natural mentors," to build their capacities in mentoring relationships.
- Effective mentoring relationships build resilience, promote engagement, and teach skills that are transferable beyond the relationship itself.
- Both mentors and mentees experience positive gains in esteem, confidence, and self-efficacy in meaningful mentoring relationships.

Chapter Four

Reinventing Reading

Making Literacy Instruction Come Alive

There can be no engaged school community without a consortium of engaged readers and writers. "Most of us can probably agree that developing students into accomplished lifelong readers is a cornerstone of learning and educational achievement, providing the means by which students gain most of their content knowledge both in and out of school," Houck and Novak (2016, p. 1) write, yet the benefits go far beyond academic domains. There is a strong relationship between literacy and financial well-being, social justice, and communications with others, and in the future, between one-half and two-thirds of all new jobs will require college degrees and high levels of literacy (Houck & Novak, 2016).

Currently, our country is failing to prepare students for this reality. Forty percent of those graduating from high school do not have the literacy skills that employers require, and more than 65 percent of fourth- and eighth-graders don't score as proficient readers. In reality, this data has not changed much for the nearly two decades since the implementation of No Child Left Behind, which was designed to heavily emphasize reading instruction (Houck & Novak, 2016).

The need for engaged literacy in schools and beyond is made more pressing by what Gallagher (2009) calls the "killing" of reading. The death of literacy and joyful reading, he believes, comes from myriad factors, such as valuing test taking over lifelong reading; requiring students to read texts that are too difficult for them; not providing deep enough instruction for students to access classic but difficult texts; not allowing enough recreational reading; and layering the reading experience with too many reading journals, sticky notes, and other ancillary tactics. All of the aforementioned take precedence over the three keys necessary to create and nurture lifelong readers: interesting books, time to read, and a place to read.

The Reading at Risk study (National Endowment for the Arts, 2004) found that, of those adults in this country who read, only 16 percent labeled themselves "frequent" or "avid" readers of literary texts, 54 percent were nonliterary readers, 21 percent were light readers, and 9 percent were moderate readers. Fram recounts a *Washington Post* story that 27 percent of the adults in this country did not read a single book of any kind during 2007 (cited in Gallagher, 2009).

Interestingly, there has been an information explosion occurring at the same time that literacy has waned. Connolly and Giouroukakis cite a 2007 study that shows that the average American receives more than 174 newspapers' worth of information a day. From 1986 to 2010, information intake by individuals increased 230 percent, yet only 26 percent of students met the benchmark for college and career literacy readiness (Connolly & Giouroukakis, 2016). Clearly, an aspect of literacy needs to include teaching students how to navigate the overwhelming array of information that comes their way each day in order to find valid, credible, and useful resources for their scholarship.

Engaging all students in reading is not an easy task. As students enter middle school, their love of reading, which usually is formed during the elementary years, often decreases because of conflicting interests. Friends, social media, sports, video games, and overall changing preferred activities all vie for middle schoolers' attention, and this only gets worse as students age. It becomes less and less cool to be a reader, and this is particularly true among boys. Social media takes precedence over reading, and developmental issues absorb preadolescents' and adolescents' energies (Kroger, 2007). Yet many educators across the country find ways not only to keep students engaged in reading but also to actually increase reading engagement during these developmental periods (Routman, 2014). By reinventing reading as it has been practiced over the decades, teachers have found strategies to invite students into next-generation literacy.

THE KEYS TO LITERACY ENGAGEMENT

Teaching Riveting Reading

Routman poses the following essential question: How can we create classrooms and schools in which all students thrive and become highly literate? The answer includes a number of practices for teachers. According to Routman, the two biggest questions teachers must ask are (1) What do I need to know in order for each learner to be engaged, to move their learning forward, and to grow them toward independence? and (2) How much and what kind of support do learners need to succeed? It is also vital that educators teach with authenticity, so that what students are learning is as meaningful as possible and the "difference between the instruction and the assessment of instruction vanishes" (Routman, 2014, p. 41).

In addition to planning with the end in mind and embedding formative assessment into all activities, Routman encourages educators to hear all voices and allow for ample student choice. Too often, student voices are ignored, marginalized, or drowned out; equally as frustrating, students may not feel empowered to speak or are afraid of the consequences if they do not provide the "right" input. Routman touts the "Optimal Learning Model" to help all students move toward confidence and independence in reading. In this model, instruction moves from teacher demonstration (modeling, reading aloud, explanation) to shared demonstration (shared reading and writing) to greater student independence in guided practice (student as worker, teacher as coach) to finally independent practice (student-initiated, -directed, and -assessed work). In planning for the literacy needs of each student, the teacher ponders questions about the learners' current levels of skill and knowledge; his or her strengths, weaknesses, and needs; what supports are necessary to maximize proficiency; and how assessment will take place (Routman, 2014).

Choice of materials is key to success. Routman (2014) defines *riveting reading* as the use of

> any text . . . that captures the heart and mind of the learner and serves as a springboard to develop stamina, interest, and knowledge that can transfer to other kinds of reading. Our job is to continually guide each student to find that riveting literature and also to expand his or her choices to include a variety of texts and genres. (p. 97)

To gain the information required to stock one's classroom with interesting texts and make appropriate suggestions for each unique group of readers, Murphy (2012) suggests conducting an interest survey with each student in the classroom; simple questions about habits, hobbies, and life aspirations populate the survey. After tallying the results of the survey, a contemporary approach is used to turn the answers into reading materials for students.

Look online for various articles. Print them, and keep them in topical binders for the students, matching each article with a predesigned question sheet that the student can complete after finishing the article. This approach to reading mimics the real-life reading that most adults do to research topics of personal utility and enjoyment. Murphy (2012) also suggests modeling how to be independent in finding answers to questions that students may have by conducting internet research for an expressed purpose.

Teachers who recognize the need for autonomy in book choices validate a crucial developmental task of childhood and adolescence; according to researchers and theorists, the shift from dependence to independence is the primary job of students in middle and high school (Brown & Knowles, 2007; Korbey, 2016; Young & Michael, 2015). As Brown and Knowles acknowledge, the effective literacy teacher will believe that it is his or her role to collaborate with students regarding their curriculum and instruction.

An important step toward riveting reading is developing a quality classroom library, and students should be involved in this endeavor. In this era of diminishing budgets, Routman advises teachers to borrow from libraries, have students bring books from home, solicit community donors, buy from low-cost book fairs, and adopt classroom reading "angels" who help fill gaps by buying to match students' requests. The importance of a literature-rich curriculum across the board cannot be ignored in this era of high-stakes testing, as many have turned away from literature to focus on nonfiction only; thus, literature must be high quality and "intense," "edgy," or "compelling" as students enter middle and secondary school (Routman, 2014).

Honoring diverse reading tastes is paramount in creating an inclusive reading environment; ensuring student interests are met and not worrying so much about *what* they are reading leads to true student engagement. Boys, for example, "like to read texts that have immediate payoff in conversations with friends" (Routman, 2014, p. 97), such as sports, comics, humor, and activity-based literature, and to ignore this preference is to risk alienating male students.

Narrow-mindedness among educators regarding book selections can be detrimental to all students (Routman, 2014). Many, especially English teachers trained in the classics, can be very judgmental about what books they consider to be appropriate for classroom activities; however, as adults, people pick books that speak to them at different points in their lives or have utility for tasks at hand, and students need to be able to do the same thing freely.

Integrating social media and technology into literacy instruction can be powerful if the exchange is interactive, such as posting blogs or classroom projects on safe sites; however, internationally, the highest-performing schools use technology less and instead devote resources to teachers' salaries and supports for floundering students. So many teachers are given the latest technology but use it in the classroom in "old-fashioned" ways (Routman, 2014).

Any literacy must have an audience and a purpose; thus, promoting the use of more shared reading, sustained time for independent reading on a daily basis, modeling how one approaches different kinds of texts efficiently, using guiding questions to prepare for a reading event, guided reading, and daily reading conferences with individual students or small groups are important aspects of ensuring reading (Routman 2014).

Sustained time for independent reading must be carefully constructed. Joy in reading can be the result of choosing just the right books and having multiple times daily for independent reading, which might be in the form of whole-class time, voluntary reading after finishing required work, free-choice reading before school, time at the beginning of classes for chosen content-related materials, or reading time (independent or with a partner) after guided reading (Routman, 2014). Guided reading occurs when the teacher leads an individual or small group of students through some aspect of reading, building on their strengths and giving support when necessary, until they are competent readers and can comprehend what they are reading silently and alone.

Being Reading Role Models

Good teachers promote "book talk" endlessly; they discuss the significant questions each text raises, as well as students' questions (Routman, 2014). Educators must be reading role models who provide ample time each day devoted to reading, and they must ensure that each student gets the personalized support and instruction needed. To maximize student engagement, these teachers use questions prior to information reading, such as asking students what they know, think, feel, and want to find out about a topic.

Educators who understand the value of encouraging engaged reading require students to come prepared to discuss by having them write notes, make concept maps, illustrate, or use other means to get ready for discussion; they encourage divergent thinking and make certain to tease out the opinions of reluctant readers (Routman, 2014). Perhaps most importantly, and regardless of what others think, teachers committed to helping students find a love for reading continue to read aloud to their students long after elementary school.

At the school level, effective literacy leadership is required. Schools need to focus on the big picture of literacy, not merely raise comprehension scores on standardized tests. Professional literacy communities and mentorship for teachers are important components of a school-wide approach, as well as having visible displays that show the value of reading. Environmental building walk-throughs can tell an outsider a great deal about the culture of a school in relation to its literacy goals; this walk can highlight messages that the school sends about the importance of reading, how literacy achievements are displayed and celebrated, what classroom expectations are for literacy, and what resources are available to all members of the school community (Routman, 2014).

In this day and age, teachers essentially must be "marketers" who sell chosen books and the very act of reading to their students (Routman, 2014). Part of selling students on books and reading is to make the story come alive. Finding the hooks or relating texts to field trips or project-based learning that has taken place in the classroom are strategies for making the book matter to students' lives (Young & Michael, 2015). Good teachers also jump on whatever titles are hot—such as the *Hunger Games* phenomenon, the Olympics, or a global event.

Bringing in multimedia components also can help with the marketing of books. Book trailers act as an excellent hook, as one can have students use technology to create their own book trailers. It is amazing how many kids want to read a book if it is preceded by a good book trailer. The use of other media types benefits students whose primary learning style may not be visual or linguistic (Gardner, 2011).

Such strategies are essential, as research demonstrates that struggling students can actually read more difficult materials if they are motivated to do so (Ivey & Broaddus, 2001). Finding inviting reading materials lies at the heart of quality classroom practice, and Ivey and Broaddus found that students who are highly motivated to read such materials as nonfiction, mysteries, reference books, series, and magazines reflect the daily habits of adults around them, more than the literature of most language arts classrooms, which include textbooks and award-winning fiction.

Aside from choosing books that individual students can relate to, it is also possible to engage small groups or the whole class in reading when relevant and engaging topics are put forth (Young & Michael, 2015). In some cases, a student may not think a book will connect to him or her, but when the overall themes are introduced in an interesting manner, the book becomes surprisingly engaging. In selecting topics that are of personal, local, or national interest to students, the teacher taps into inherent motivation to read to find out more; however, this also entails tackling difficult or controversial topics at times, if reading is to be authentic (Ivey & Broaddus, 2001).

Norton and Norton (2011) promote the use of books on sensitive topics; however, it is important for educators to (1) consider the controversy for the school community; (2) determine the author's point of view, the positive attributes of the book, and the possible negative reactions; (3) ensure the book meets all standards for quality literature and is not chosen merely for the high interest resulting from its controversy; (4) be able to articulate why the book was chosen; and (5) be able to discuss both sides of the censorship question intelligently.

Teachers often have success introducing difficult but engaging topics before beginning a book. If, for example, a class is going to read *Where the Red Fern Grows* (Rawls, 1961), the teacher might start the unit by posing such questions as

- Why do kids fall in love with animals?
- How much would you work to buy the pet of your choice?
- How do you show your love for your pet?

By involving students in these discussions, educators prepare their pupils for deep immersion in the story; additionally, when reading about disheartening subjects, such as hunger or poverty, teachers can encourage students to generate ways that they might better the situation through their individual or collective actions (Norton & Norton, 2011).

Providing Daily Time to Read

Even when a teacher is able to practice these strategies to increase reading engagement, it is essential that students be afforded regular time designated for reading. With a seeming tsunami of mandated initiatives overtaking the classroom teacher, how does one find time to the justify the philosophy of dedicated reading time espoused by quality literacy experts? Ivey and Broaddus's study on the motivating features of reading instruction highlight the importance of dedicated reading time. From a survey of 1,765 students across 23 schools, it was found that students prefer silent reading time and teacher read-alouds more than any other reading activities (Ivey & Broaddus, 2001).

Students are motivated by having a choice in reading materials and read a far more diverse range of materials outside of school rather than in school (Ivey & Broaddus, 2001). If middle school teachers want to maximize independent reading experiences, they must value reading solely for pleasure during these time periods, and they must embrace student choice about the reading materials. After students select books that interest or excite them, they need time to read these books. As teachers note, there is always a decision to make regarding class time, including finding time for independent reading and incorporating it into daily lessons.

Involving Families and Community

Even the best and most dedicated educators still grapple with how to engage families and the larger community in literacy, as schools and teachers need involvement and reinforcement of literacy beyond their classroom walls (Grant & Ray, 2016; Mapp & Kuttner, 2013). Families and communities are busy with many responsibilities and issues, and becoming involved directly in literacy activities is not often their top priority; however, when teachers are able to engage families or communities, the impact on student literacy is highly profitable.

If educators want a literacy initiative to be a success, it is best to involve students as leaders right from the start and have them engage their parents in the recruitment and planning process (Epstein, 2011; Ferlazzo & Hammond, 2009). Inviting all families into literacy development is particularly important when there are subcommunities who may be marginalized in the educational process. These include minority communities, new immigrants, students with disabilities, or families for whom English is not the primary language of the home; it also might include parents with low levels of literacy themselves. Family literacy programs aim to create safe, welcoming, and doable programs that invite children, their families, and community partners into a collaboration that leads to a more literate lifetime for all (Epstein, 2011).

Developing Family Literacy Programs

Simply put, family literacy programs are approaches to education in which parents and children learn and grow together, and there are multiple, mutually supportive goals, including addressing the literacy strengths and needs of the family or community while promoting adults' involvement in children's education and recognizing adults as a powerful influence on children's academic success. As there is a reciprocal nature in parent–child relationships, successful programs include both parent-initiated and child-initiated activities to build and nurture the development of those relationships and to increase both parties' motivation to learn (Family Literacy, 2015).

Many family literacy programs integrate both early childhood and adult-focused education in their initiatives; thus, effective programs provide interactive literacy activities for family members and their children; education for parents to facilitate their children's learning and become full partners in their education; parent literacy training that can lead to economic self-sufficiency and meet adults' literacy goals; age-appropriate education to prepare children for success in school and life experiences; and such resources as books, activity bags, and other materials to be used in the home (Family Literacy, 2015).

While school is the obvious first stage for literacy development, home and community are no less essential in the formation of fluent readers. Strong partnerships among all parties set the tone for promoting the importance of lifelong reading. Effective partnerships can be formed, and strategies, activities, and habits can be successful in creating and nurturing reading habits that last long beyond formal school years (Family Literacy, 2015).

Helping Parents Understand the Reading Process

While teachers have had direct instruction in the reading process, it is rare for family members to be well-informed, yet a key to being able to nurture struggling readers is a firm grasp of the process of reading itself (Young, Jean, & Mead, 2018). The more that family members understand the components of reading, such as phonemic awareness, phonics, fluency, vocabulary, and comprehension, and what aspects their child is struggling with, the more they can work at home to augment the weaker areas while using his or her competencies. Educators should help families seek out specific information and help them to feel comfortable enough to ask questions so that they understand how best to address areas of need at home (Grant & Ray, 2016). If reading assignments and homework consistently seem too hard, families should ask teachers to make sure that assigned work is at the correct developmental level. Kittle (2013) believes that the language of what students are reading must be accessible, as that makes reading more enjoyable and increases the likelihood of persisting, even if a text is difficult.

Schools must work with parents so that they feel empowered to ask the questions necessary to be active and effective helpers in their children's literacy education. For example, in addition to identifying and discussing each child's strengths and interests, teachers should share the child's profile of reading skills and discuss worries or concerns, have clear strategies to address those concerns, be able to clarify the reading instruction program being used, and discuss collaborative next steps to best assist the child in and out of school (WGBH Educational Foundation, 2002).

Connecting Reading and Writing

For many years, reading and writing were seen as such separate processes that they were taught independently. Recent research, however, demonstrates that they are far more interdependent than once was believed. Struggling readers can improve literacy through their writing (Graham & Hebert, 2010; Young, Noonan, & Bonanno-Sotiropoulos, 2018). An extensive study conducted by the Carnegie Corporation found that writing is too frequently an underutilized tool for improving reading skills and content learning (Graham & Hebert, 2010).

Three primary strategies improve literacy through writing: having students write about what they are reading, teaching students the skills to produce the texts that they are reading, and increasing the amount of writing that students do (Graham & Hebert, 2010). In the best of learning partnerships, family involvement in the writing process augments what happens in schools and cements the relationship between the two processes.

Routman also stresses the natural marriage of reading and writing in literacy instruction, imploring teachers to set aside daily periods of 10 to 20 minutes to "just write." In these sessions, teachers must focus on the process rather than trying to integrate instruction; they should also make judicious use of modeling while demonstrating the writing process. Editing and refining occur in later steps. It is important to have students publish their writing frequently and for teachers to use read-alouds, guided reading, shared writing, and other opportunities to illustrate what writers do with regard to their craft (Routman, 2014; Young et al., 2018).

There are multiple meaningful ways to capitalize on natural needs for writing, such as thank-you notes for gifts received, requests for products or services, letters to the editor, communications with friends or family members at a distance, travel diaries, and journals. There also are ways of personalizing reading responses, such as keeping reading logs, responding to favorite books, or writing to beloved characters or authors. Students can be helped to write their own books and then read them aloud, students can write books to share with younger students, or families can pen their family histories. Younger students can dictate their stories to older ones and then share them in reading partnerships. Anything that personalizes the reading and writing experience improves engagement in the process.

A collection of strategies for bridging out-of-school literacies with classroom practice highlights some of the innovative activities occurring around the country; for example, young students from the United States might be involved in a project that links them with students in Russia, or an after-school computer club might target students at risk for reading and writing failures in school and engage them in computer games designed to advance their learning. This highly engaging form of writing and responding has been shown to increase motivation to write, length of writing, and reading skills (Hull & Schultz, 2002).

Developing Rich Vocabularies

Vocabulary skills vary widely among students. For some, oral vocabulary is an area of great strength, yet for those who struggle with language and reading, actively building a rich vocabulary can ease the reading struggle (Bergland, 2014; Butler et al., 2010; Wiener, 1988). When children have delayed language, parents naturally to tend to talk less to them; however, while some reduction of language may be helpful, all children need good stimulation and the opportunity to build their vocabulary bank.

Wiener (1988) emphasizes the importance of informal, unstructured conversation to spark children's learning. All parents should talk while they are doing things with their children to enhance their vocabulary and concepts.

When parents make their thinking and actions visible, the dialogue strengthens the child's vocabulary, as does modeling an interest in words, their meanings, and their uses (Bergland, 2014; Butler et al., 2010).

Children with vocabulary deficits are especially vulnerable as they become readers in middle school, with a steep increase in the level of vocabulary used in texts around the fourth grade (Butler et al., 2010; Spear-Swerling, 2006). Parents should discuss their children's vocabulary assessments with classroom teachers and specialists to determine if targeted instruction in vocabulary is warranted and what strategies can be used at home to complement classroom activities (Butler et al., 2010). New technologies, including electronic and online resources, can also prove valuable.

Finding Strategies for Success

There are many alternative ways to help readers who wrestle with decoding, reading retention, or comprehension. These approaches are particularly helpful at home; for example, readers with memory problems can be taught memory aids, such as mnemonics, and students with comprehension problems can use sticky notes to record seminal information about what they are reading (Young, Bonanno-Sotiropoulos, & Smolinski, 2018). These techniques for families do not require advanced training; they can be as simple as reading aloud daily or playing boxed or online word games. Drop Everything and Read (D.E.A.R.; HarperCollins Publishers, 2018) can be done at home, so that parents and others are modeling good reading habits; students can "teach" family members what they learn when they read or dramatize their selections.

It cannot be said enough: Forming a strong, positive relationship with a child's teachers and specialists is the key to using the most effective accommodations and strategies for each reader. Families can ask for computer programs or sites that target their child's reading needs; they can also ask for suggestions for enhancing vocabulary, as a rich vocabulary aids in reading success. However, it is often beneficial for educators to take the first step and send home such a list, as families often do not know to ask or exactly what they should be asking for.

Most struggling readers are visual or kinesthetic learners; thus, Quick, Hocevar, and Zimmer (2014) recommend the use of visual literacy strategies so that students can use their strengths during reading tasks, such as graphic organizers that can help them with topics, main ideas, details, sequential order of items, relationships among things, story elements, and similarities and differences. Students can use elaboration (colors, designs, or personal pictures) to aid memory or personalization (creating associations to information with personal pictures or designs that make sense to the reader) to enhance the reading process (Quick et al., 2014).

Using Technology Wisely

Quick et al. promote the use of technology to support literacy initiatives, given that contemporary students are adept at its use; however, as part of any literacy program, the authors push for direct instruction in information literacy strategies. Too many students consume large amounts of information without having the knowledge to differentiate between what is useful and what is not credible. Beyond didactic instruction on how to navigate the web, students need to understand whether the information they find is valid. Students need to learn to ask themselves (1) Who sponsors the site? (2) Who is the author of the information, and what are his or her credentials? (3) What is the site's purpose? (4) Is the information accurate and well written? and (5) Is the information current? (Quick et al., 2014). Connolly and Giouroukakis (2016) reiterate that being literate in contemporary society means that "our students must be able to think, create, critique, question and communicate effectively using the semiotic forms they encounter daily" (p. 103). This includes efficiently acquiring information online, analyzing the validity and usefulness of the information, and incorporating good information into a variety of presentations, both online and off-line.

A plethora of enjoyable ways to integrate technology into the classroom exists, including having evidence scavenger hunts, creating bulletin board displays, and using online programs to create flipbooks (Connolly & Giouroukakis, 2016). Access to virtual libraries (a safe venue for communicating reading interests with others), free electronic books, and networking with others over what students are reading and how they react to their reading are just a few ways the internet has increased the availability of reading and writing activities.

Approaching Standardized Testing Creatively

Connolly and Giouroukakis (2016) urge teachers to approach the required and much-dreaded standardized testing routine with creativity and purpose. Using backward planning, in which teachers move from three seminal questions (What are the desired results? What is evidence of students' understanding? What learning experiences and instruction will best enable students to achieve the results?) into challenging and engaging lessons aligned with next-generation literacy assessments, guides the work (Wiggins & McTighe, 2011). Rather than bemoaning the presence of testing, Connolly and Giouroukakis (2016) propose that teachers view the latest thrust of assessment—reading multiple complex texts independently and analyzing them using evidence or rationales for student answers—as a jumping-off point for working with historical documents, complex texts, and global issues.

Service learning is one of the deeper learning strategies that engage students in building content knowledge. Students are more apt to pay attention and write in a more connected manner when they believe that their work can make a difference. Myriad methods of engagement eschew "drill and kill" and instead focus on students choosing to tackle real-life topics of importance and developing their campaigns using articles, websites, video talks, and debates; writing formal proposals; creating flyers; and constructing ads (Connolly & Giouroukakis, 2016).

All children have an intrinsic desire to help others; thus, when they have a purpose and know that others are depending on them and their research, literacy work takes on primacy, as it is seen as a means to address a genuine need. Along the way, students master content and research skills as well as learn about the subtleties of persuasive language, debate, and how to convince an audience. They explore their subject matter through discourse, considering their own perspectives on the information and analyzing how others communicate. These kinds of authentic activities make literacy learning "stick" because students are invested in meaningful outcomes derived from their efforts (Connolly & Giouroukakis, 2016).

Mentoring

Struggling or disengaged readers may benefit greatly from a reading buddy or mentor. Such national programs as the Read, Think, Share mentoring program matches students from low-income backgrounds with college student mentors. The students and mentors read books and discuss them online together in a secure forum. Students can select books from a wide range of titles that suit their personal interests. The program gives the students positive feedback and academic support, as well as the gift of corresponding with strong role models. While the primary goal is to build core skills in writing and reading, mentors also are intent on building social skills and connections through their relationships (Reader to Reader, n.d.).

Schools can set up their own peer-mentoring programs. Mentors must demonstrate academic achievement, social skills, community involvement, and diversity, as well as the potential to inspire students who are at risk. The mentors can relate to their mentees in ways that differ from the way teachers and other adults relate to them, given that they are young adults themselves. These programs involve older students forming friendships with and mentoring younger children in a structured environment. Cross-age peer programs provide growth and learning opportunities for both mentors and mentees, resulting in gains for both. Such programs recognize the importance of peer relationships for children and adolescents. These programs take advantage of children's increasing interest in peer friendships as they enter the middle school and secondary school years; however, younger children who are reluctant readers also thrive in relationships with "reading buddies" who act as informal mentors. Mentees' natural tendency to look up to slightly older youth means that they view their mentor as a role model and someone worth listening to. Equally important, peer mentors benefit from interacting with each other in positive ways through the volunteer experience, often building new relationships beyond their normal circle of friends (Belotti, 2016).

There are additional outcomes beyond simply reading gains. Peer mentors also can support their mentees as they go through transitions in their lives. As Garringer and MacRae (2008) point out, mentees in elementary or middle school benefit from having an older student help them with such challenges as moving to a new school and the accompanying changes in social relationships, while mentoring secondary students can be extremely valuable in helping with career and postsecondary educational decisions.

Older students, even those who may not be highly proficient readers, can be effective reading buddies for younger students and students with reading disabilities. In turn, this can boost their self-esteem and interest in becoming more proficient readers (Belotti, 2016). Reading-mentor programs can also use new technologies, such as online programs. This is particularly crucial for rural areas or programs that lack the availability of face-to-face mentors. One program, for example, motivates Native American youths while connecting them to college-age mentors 3,000 miles away (Reader to Reader, n.d.).

Schools may also use community and business members as mentors, either in school or by creating innovative, on-site programs. In one study, mentoring school-aged readers had powerful benefits for both the mentors and mentees (Tracey, Hornery, Seaton, Craven, & Yeung, 2014). Specific matches—such as a male reading mentor with a boy who does not have a father in the home—can fill developmental needs, as well.

Closing the Reading Gender Gap

By the middle school grades, boys lag seriously behind girls in their literacy achievements. Because boys are less verbal than girls, the contemporary, standards-based curricula now required of all schools can doom boys as early as fourth or fifth grade. One result of this disparity in performance is an image in boys' minds that they are not as proficient in reading as girls are, thus leading them to disengage from reading and writing at an early age (Jacobsen, 2014).

Gender differences in how students see reading necessitates that we approach their instruction differently. According to Jacobson, girls want to relate to the books' characters and find reading fiction a pleasure, while boys want to be able to immediately use what they read. Boys need to see a purpose for what they are reading, and they need a real-world use for the text. Starting in early middle school, boys most enjoy reading "magazines, graphic novels, and books that feature gory scenes or gross humor" (Jacobsen, 2014, p. 4).

Smith and Wilhelm (2002) explore some of the basic reasons for boys' struggles with literacy, especially as they move into middle school and beyond. It is a well-established fact that boys underperform on measures of literacy as compared to girls, but the reasons for their low achievement still are hotly debated (Jacobsen, 2014). A review of research and statistics shows that boys take longer to learn to read than do girls. They read less and have a lower performance rate in comprehension of narrative and expository texts, and they have lower estimations of their reading ability, value reading less, and have a reduced interest in leisure reading. Boys spend less time reading, enjoy it less, and are more apt to label themselves as "nonreaders" (Smith & Wilhelm, 2002).

One culprit may be the "feminization of reading," in which reading and other literate undertakings are seen as "sissified." In this society, to be masculine is to be competent, so boys will go to great lengths to avoid things at which they do not excel. This is particularly true if the activities involve effort that could lead to failure; however, meta-analysis of research on gender and reading demonstrates that boys may simply like to read things that most English teachers do not see as standard academic fare. Boys tend to gravitate toward informational texts, graphic novels and comic books, magazines and newspaper articles, and electronic texts more than girls do; they like escapism and humor more; choose to read about things they like to do, such as hobbies or sports; and enjoy collecting things, like series of books by the same author or on the same topic. They are better at information retrieval and work-related literacy activities than are girls. Boys are less likely to talk about books but prefer active responses to their reading (Smith & Wilhelm, 2002).

Jacobsen (2014) suggests that one must adopt different strategies in order to entice boys to read. These include using the kinds of reading that boys value and enjoy, demonstrating the utility of what they are reading, and involving their fathers or other valued male figures or role models in literacy activities.

Reducing the Need for Intervention

Allen reports on an interesting trend in developing the literacy intervention classroom. A small classroom, no more than 14 students, was created for students who were only a year or two below grade level and did not have behavioral problems. It was designed to accelerate student achievement, provide targeted supports, and bolster stamina and fluency, with the end goal of reading and writing proficiency. Students worked with the same teacher all day (with the exception of outside activities) and stayed one to two years, depending on their progress. With an expert teacher and using a workshop approach, students participated daily in guided literature groups, writer's workshops, word study, independent reading, and read-alouds. They were exposed to a rich literacy program using a variety of texts matched to their reading levels and individual interests. A well-developed in-class library filled with "riveting reading" supplemented the regular school library. Working across all content areas, the teacher employed such things as visual and graphic organizers, and parents were expected to participate in a home reading program. Large blocks of literacy instruction time were necessary so that direct intervention was not disrupted; however, students had daily push-in for math and took part in activities outside of the classroom (Allen, 2016).

Students were selected for the literacy intervention classroom based on these criteria: a reading aptitude near grade level, excellent attendance, no major guidance or behavioral issues, parental commitment to involvement, and a socioeconomic status mix that matched the school as a whole. The year began with a month-long boot camp to teach the tools that students would use during reading workshop; however, topics, investigations, and book choices were developed out of student interest and excitement. Ongoing assessment throughout the year was frequent and authentic and seemed to demonstrate powerful success over the years (Allen, 2016).

Routman also pushes for a reduction in the need for reading intervention yet emphasizes prevention rather than remediation as the first line of defense. This involves investing in excellent kindergarten literacy instruction through universal teaching. Studies have shown that nearly 100 percent of students can be reading at grade level by the end of first or second grade if early instruction takes place in a high-quality preschool, early tutoring, superior kindergarten, and such proven programs as Reading Recovery (Reading Recovery, 2018; Routman, 2014). All these interventions cost money; however, the argument for this early expenditure is that reaching literacy acumen in early childhood is much less costly and debilitating than trying to remediate later (Reading Recovery, 2018).

Valuing Variety

For many, there is the belief that only "quality literature counts" when it comes to reading. Instead, it is essential that struggling readers see that all of their efforts at literacy are of value. This means that finding engaging material is paramount for enticing young people to read. Smith and Wilhelm interviewed young male readers and found that they overwhelmingly agreed that, if it was interesting, they would read it. These same young men gave only scant time to texts before they rejected them; for this reason, the authors note the qualities that attracted boys to the act of reading, such as music as text—a favorite form of "reading" for boys. Finding "ways to use music and other popular cultural materials as a bridge to developing more canonical literacies" (Smith & Wilhelm, 2002, p. 150) encompasses all reluctant readers. Reluctant readers enjoy texts that are storied, are visual, are in a series by the same author or involve the same characters, and have a predictability of style (Reading Recovery, 2018).

Finding high-interest reading material is key for all reluctant readers, and children should be given as much freedom as possible to read what they want to read, not what adults think they should read (Scieszka, cited in Gallagher, 2009). An expanded definition of *reading* is necessary, as well as putting a stop to the demonization of other media, as they are not the "bad guy. Those things aren't going away. I think we did ourselves a disservice in the past by saying TV is bad, reading is good. It's not that cut and dried" (Scieszka, cited in Gallagher, 2009, p. 84).

Smith and Wilhelm stress that teachers and parents must rethink the definitions of *literacy* to be "aware of the digital literacies ... students use, want to use, and often need to be able to use outside of school." Further, educators "need to find ways to integrate the study of literature with electronic and popular cultural texts. Doing so will engage students with new ways of knowing, reading, and writing that build on and expand those they already know" (Smith & Wilhelm, 2006, p. 168). One benefit of this approach is that students can teach their parents and teachers about their technoliteracies, showing them how they can learn best.

As far back as 2002, Alvermann argued that both teachers and parents need to openly embrace a rapidly changing digital world. While the flood of digital information into classrooms and homes may threaten the "knowledge authority" of teachers and parents, the digital trend is continually growing; thus, adults had better learn to be more tech savvy and enter the worlds of children and adolescents in order to engage them in the "new literacies" (Alvermann, 2002).

Continuing Family Engagement with Literacy

The largest such survey of American reading ever conducted found "calamitous, universal falling off of reading" at about age 13, and this drop-off persists throughout students' lives (cited in Gallagher, 2009, p. 112). The same survey reported radical changes in the way reading is experienced in current students' lives (National Endowment for the Arts, 2004).

This first generation of students, often called digital natives, has been surrounded by electronic media from birth, read less, and read less well than previous generations. The kind of reading that they do via the internet is not complex and tends toward headline, blurb, and blog type of reading. These factors lead to students whose school performance is lacking, as is their engagement in civil life. In the past decade, the reading proficiency of college graduates fell 23 percent. Half of the adults in the United States do not read nor do they read to their children, and 55 percent of those who read below a basic level are unemployed (Gallagher, 2009).

It is unfortunate that most families become less involved in literacy activities with their children after they reach middle school. Beers reports that middle school readers recalled many reading activities within their families, dating back to their earliest memories. Students fondly remember prolonged reading, reading aloud with their parents, parents modeling reading activities, the presence of a "home library," having books and other reading materials in their cars or at appointments or on vacations, and hearing bedtime stories. When interviewed, the parents in this study also recalled these activities and said that, if they needed childcare for their children, they looked for venues in which literacy activities were an integral part of the curriculum. They also remembered that, when their children began school, they already viewed reading as valuable and pleasurable (Beers, 2005).

A 2014 study by Scholastic revealed that of the 1,000 children surveyed, 40 percent (or 4 in 10) "say they wished their parents had continued reading aloud to them" (p. 6). Some parents may find it awkward to continue the read-aloud tradition with older children, but it is crucial that they find new ways to keep family literacy a priority. Parents still should read aloud with their children until there is active resistance; at that point, older children can practice their reading by sharing with younger siblings. Other media, such as movies, videos, and documentaries, can also serve as springboards for awakening interest in older students; they can compare and contrast a book and its movie adaptation, create blogs and multimedia presentations of their own, and discuss their reactions to shared family television viewing (Scholastic, 2014).

Smith and Wilhelm (2006) found that older children were far more motivated to read texts that were "exportable"—that could easily be exported into a conversation. Such exportable texts can be as simple as sports updates, headlines, financial information, movie reviews, or weather stories and can be derived from print or from digital means. If a shared interest exists with another family member or friend, it can spur interest in reading for informational purposes; this is particularly true for reluctant readers and boys. Skillful parents and teachers can then extend the reading experience by suggesting biographies or autobiographies of favorite players, memoirs of a particular season, sports analyses, magazines, or blogs. Having subscriptions (print or online) to magazines of interest also helps to engage older readers.

Families and community members need to stay the course with middle school and secondary students as far as literacy efforts are concerned. With middle school students, Baigelman (2014) suggests that family members help young adolescents find reading that they will like; refrain from criticizing choices, even if they are not parental favorites; and encourage reluctant readers by allowing them to have choice and control over what they read.

Another valuable strategy is to continue to model reading and read together but switch to parallel reading rather than reading the same book aloud. Other strategies include offering praise for any small steps toward progress, giving books as gifts, choosing books that relate to students' current passions and interests, and finding ways to help middle schoolers and secondary students see how reading can be linked to their passions in real life. Families also should engage in adult-like discussions with their children when talking about what they are reading. Finally, adults can use a child's interest in social media to extend his or her reading, often with the student leading the way by demonstrating the latest technologies to the parents (Baigelman, 2014).

Transcescent students and teens who struggle with reading rarely want to just sit down and read; thus, reading needs to be tied to more active and interactive experiences. It is also important for reluctant readers to find series by the same author or books clustered on a particular topic, so that preknowledge and anticipation can ease reading difficulties (Baigelman, 2014).

Meeting with parents and holding conversations about reading is a major component of classrooms in which literacy is an expectation; teachers can share observations about a student's reading habits, strengths and needs, and particular interests, making suggestions about the kind of books their child would be drawn to (Baigelman, 2014). In many cases, families simply need to be reminded that they still play a key role in promoting their children's literacy, as they frequently assume that their early adolescents' desire for greater independence means that they no longer need be involved in reading with them. During family literacy meetings, teachers can share tips and websites that provide information pertinent to middle and high school literacy.

Scholastic (2015) offers excellent suggestions for families of preadolescent and adolescent readers, such as continuing to read aloud with middle school students who may benefit from shared reading or siblings who read to each other. Scholastic also recommends modeling reading, keeping interesting reading materials in the home, setting limits on television and computer time to free up time for reading, talking about what family members are reading, and leaving time in preadolescents' busy schedules to just relax and read materials of their own choosing.

Moving beyond conversations and including families in actual literacy-centered activities is the next stage of engagement (Scholastic, 2015). In family literacy conferences, a savvy teacher should discuss methods for increasing family participation in literacy. Schools and families can also join forces for such events as book fairs, community book swaps, and events held at local bookstores and sponsors. Students and parents should be tapped to plan events whenever possible.

Tapping into Available Resources

If the local school and community do not offer family literacy opportunities, it is possible for families and community members to plan their own. It is not necessary to be a reading specialist to promote fun-filled activities based around literacy activities; for example, Scholastic (2018) offers a downloadable facilitator's guide for planning a Read and Rise Family Reading Night, in which one part engages parents and family members in an interactive discussion about how to use everyday activities to build children's literacy skills and the other part encourages families to work together to create their own original books, which they can take home with them.

Drawing on local knowledge and traditions, as well as partnering with local agencies, school and family members can cooperate in developing activities that make the most sense for their communities, such as book exchanges and enlisting artists and sports teams to speak to children in order to hook and support young readers (Laviolette, 2016). Businesses might donate a portion of sales to a nonprofit, thus combining entrepreneurship with socially responsible sales. There are many examples of such partnerships:

- The New York Knicks promotes reading via interactive videos and the internet through Read to Achieve program; successful readers earn team gear and tickets to games, while older students can participate in the Knicks Poetry Slam, which capitalizes on the popularity of hip-hop and poetry.
- The Boston Celtics reaches out to empower children who are blind at 45 local schools through collaboration with the National Braille Press. Some of these resources may be particularly helpful in reaching middle and high school boys who are drawn to such activities as sports and music but are reluctant readers (Celtics, 2014).
- Six Flags Amusement Park, Great Escape, sponsors a summer reading challenge for local students. After students document their daily summer reading, they are eligible for a free day at the amusement park (Six Flags, 2017).
- Local or chain grocery stores often donate the necessities for a community reading celebration party or cookout.

Using Local and National Resources

Since 1967, September 8 has been designated as International Literacy Day (International Literacy Association, 2018). Ideas for community–school engagement include service activities, such as holding a book drive for charity, donating children's books to an organization, or starting a reading club with an international theme. These can also be woven into school community service requirements or badge activities.

The National Education Association proudly sponsors Read across America Day, which is celebrated on March 2 (author Theodor Geisel's birthday) or the closest school day to that date (National Education Association, 2017). Each school or community is free to plan its own celebration; however, there are ideas and resources listed online that can facilitate such planning.

The National Center for Families Learning (2018) provides a website with ideas for keeping families engaged in literacy activities, such as holding a family–school reading day (or days) in which family members are invited to school to read favorite stories, learn about games and tools, and brainstorm ways to stay engaged in the reading process throughout the year. The organization also notes that having books for families to take home, as well as certificates of participation, is a good incentive for the activities. Local bookstores and other businesses can be solicited to donate books and bookmarks.

The National Center for Learning Disabilities (n.d.) offers a simple Home Literacy Environment Checklist that can help families gauge the "friendliness" of their home for supporting children's literacy as well as numerous websites to enhance family literacy.

Celebrating Literacy Achievements

Encouragement also involves celebrating the successes of readers, especially those who are reluctant or struggling. The Southwest Educational Development Laboratory (SEDL, 2005) notes that "students who struggle with reading need consistent feedback on their efforts" (p. 15). The report further states that "the non-tangible incentives of teacher praise and constructive feedback have proven more motivational than the tangible rewards" (p. 16), although tangible rewards, such as competitions and other activities, can spur reading as well.

Blow (2011) stresses that bribery rarely works to motivate students; however, positive reinforcement goes far, as self-esteem is a need for all students. As an example, a "Got Caught Reading" wall outside the classroom door, replete with artfully displayed pictures of students who read specific books and gave opinions and reports on them, serves as a reminder to all students about the importance of reading.

To raise the status of reading and other literacy activities, schools and communities need to emphasize the celebration of reading success as much as they recognize athletic or academic achievements (Blow, 2011). This might involve local media publicizing the reading achievements of students or recognizing the efforts of reading mentors and community members who support reading efforts.

Schools can plan celebratory events, such as a "Book Blast & Bar-B-Que [*sic*]" as one superintendent does. This event is held in August to recognize K–8 students who have met summer reading challenges. Students, family, and community members eat, dance, and celebrate the act of reading (TeachThought, 2018).

Using Books to Promote Prosocial Development

Reading quality, appropriately chosen literature can help students address transitions and developmental or life challenges (Dirks, 2010). Discovering how fictitious and true characters have faced their own personal problems and challenges can assist students of all ages in solving their own. Tu (1999) stresses that, not only can literature help children understand that they are not alone in encountering problems, but it is also able to help teachers and family members understand and relate to students' feelings about these problems.

The use of appropriate reading experiences as "bibliotherapy" has been integrated into counseling and culturally responsive pedagogy (Dirks, 2010; Tatum, 2005). Skillful teachers need to integrate readings from such fields as education, sociology, psychology, anthropology, and social work into their instruction (Tatum, 2005). The same can be true for family and community reading, as right reading choices can help children through such experiences as the loss of a beloved family member or pet or the preparation for adolescence or high school (Dirks, 2010). Reading also can normalize some of the aspects of having a disability, such as anxiety or depression.

As early as the 1950s, educators argued for the effectiveness of using books to help people understand their problems; "it allows the reader to identify with a character and realize that he or she is not the only person with a particular problem. As the character works through a problem, the reader is emotionally involved in the struggle and ultimately achieves insight about his or her own situation (Shrodes, 1955, p. 24). This can be particularly powerful for children and adolescents feeling isolated or struggling due to a learning disability, being part of a marginalized group, struggling with gender identification, or having a parent in the military (Dirks, 2010).

Books clearly can be used outside of a strictly clinical setting. Choosing readings for a child or adolescent or creating reading groups around particular books or topics of developmental importance is something that educators and parents can do (Dirks, 2010). Librarians, reading specialists, and classroom teachers have valuable suggestions for each particular student.

Families should feel free to approach librarians and teachers, as their children need the guidance that books can provide; the reverse can also happen if teachers observe or children share life problems. Tu (1999) proposes that the literature that holds the most power to assist children through developmental passages must be well written and developmentally appropriate, honest in its portrayal of the situation, present multidimensional characters, provide problem-solving strategies, offer the potential for controversy, and avoid easy or pat solutions.

According to Crippen (2012), reading helps children develop cultural identity, encourages creativity, and fosters social and personal development. Quality children's literature can foster social development by creating characters who may express values and beliefs different from the reader's own; this encourages children to understand others' worldviews and become more likely to accept diverse opinions and backgrounds. The act of reading itself allows students to develop relationships with other people, encouraging greater social contact (Dirks, 2010).

Books can promote prosocial development in powerful ways that can benefit individuals, families, schools, and communities; for example, a program where adolescents work with adult partners in collaborative writing projects aimed at helping the students write their way through life struggles and learn problem-solving and life-planning skills with foundations in hope for the future. Students read and present their works and collaborate with their adult partners in articulating their life plans (Hull & Schultz, 2002). The interactive relationship among speaking, reading, and writing offers opportunities for accelerating positive development while simultaneously developing literacy skills (Dirks, 2010).

Turning Reading into Action

Showing students myriad ways that reading can provide the data for personal or social action is a key toward increasing its value. Vygotsky (1962) saw all learning as relational and social, writing that people learn best when they are addressing an issue or solving a problem that is of personal interest and importance. Once meaningful topics are identified, struggling readers can be helped to use writing or other means of expression to address their concerns; reading then becomes the logical avenue for informing themselves, so that they can write a letter to the editor, make a proposal to their school, express gratitude, or plan a family trip (Crippen, 2012).

A genuine need for inquiry is the best motivator. This might be found in instructions, recipes, how-to guides, football playbooks, or travel brochures. It's hard to imagine a teenager who doesn't want to read a driver's manual in order to get his or her license; thus, reading that has a clear purpose is more likely to engage reluctant readers.

Reading can also be the springboard for social action. Reluctant readers may read in order to help others. Family and students can read about various charitable organizations that promote reading in order to pick the recipient of their fund or donation drive. National nonprofits like Milk and Bookies, United through Reading, or Pajama Program help underserved students, the homeless, and veterans (Laviolette, 2016).

FINAL THOUGHTS

Public recognition of reading needs to be raised to the same level of recognition as sports, arts, and academic accomplishments. Because reading is crucial to both academic and career success, as well as to the development of one's sense of self and inner life, marginalized readers need to be invited into the tradition of literacy and see their progress rewarded in a manner that reflects the value placed on other school activities. Teachers and students must imagine a day when there is a readers' awards banquet equal to that of the annual sports awards celebration. By using the strategies suggested by researchers and the accomplished teachers featured throughout this chapter, schools, parents, and communities can recruit and engage reluctant middle school readers while keeping previously invested readers on the path of continued advancement throughout early adolescence.

With so many students at risk for being reluctant, nonfluent, or nonreaders, schools, families, and communities must collaborate in using proven strategies to enhance literacy while creating new activities and traditions that are unique to their localities. Home-, school-, and community-based events and practices reinforce the goal of fluency for all. In this age of new technologies, new technoliteracies have been created. Teachers and parents need to embrace these novel literacies and expand their notions of reading and literature if they are to entice today's youth into seeing themselves as readers and finding a purpose for their reading.

The school–home connection can be a particularly powerful one. Parents need to see their roles in the reading partnership as lasting well beyond the elementary school years, although their strategies in supporting struggling readers will change. In addition to learning the specifics of their children's reading profiles, families can provide teachers valuable information about their children's interests and passions. In some cases, engagement in their children's literacy may spur parents to improve their own.

Community agencies and local businesses can initiate or support ongoing literacy activities by opening their doors to families through such activities as author readings, book drives, and book clubs. They can donate labor, money, publicity, food, or prizes to events that celebrate reading successes. Using one's agency or business to promote family literacy models socially responsible practices in school, such as community service or service learning activities that center on reading.

Modeling and providing the tools for reading success are key to winning the literacy battle. If parents want children to be readers, they must be readers themselves. If schools want skilled readers, they must embrace the new literacies and technologies that are part of students' lives. And if communities want a literate citizenry, they must put books and other materials in the hands of those who do not have them, provide interesting spaces to host literacy events, and make literacy events as integral to community life as other beloved traditions and celebrations.

POINTS TO REMEMBER

- Addressing the literacy needs of all readers takes a collaboration among school, community, and family members.
- Family engagement in the reading process tends to drop off as students enter middle school; however, family members need to find alternate ways of staying involved in literacy activities with their children even as they enter adolescence.
- There must be a broader definition of *appropriate reading materials* to include a wide variety of print and multimedia sources if we are to engage all readers.

- Adults must recognize the synergistic nature of reading, writing, and speaking in creating engaging literacy programs.
- Mentors—peer, college student, or community—are powerful partners in helping struggling readers to become fluent.
- Parents and teachers should approach all struggling readers from a strengths-based approach, identifying and using students' assets and interests to promote literacy efforts.
- Quality reading, writing, and speaking experiences can promote positive development, civic engagement, and student self-efficacy.
- Every day must allow time for quality reading in a variety of forms, including independent reading of sources of a student's choosing.
- Teachers must market books in the classroom to pique students' interest in reading, and equally important, matching students' personal interests with specific books will help hook students.
- Communication between education professionals and families regarding literacy and the creation of extended learning experiences also can improve students' literacy.
- The achievements of all readers, especially those who are reluctant or struggling, must be celebrated.
- New technologies must be embraced as part of a contemporary literacy program.
- High-stakes testing and other assessments can be used to drive meaningful and engaging literacy activities to promote achievement.

Chapter Five

Instructional Practices That Make a Difference

Engaging Students in the Classroom

Student engagement can be described as the behavioral, emotional, and cognitive involvement in academic activities (Stephens, 2015). Students who are engaged in their education are more likely to demonstrate an increase in effort, attention, and social skills and experience more positive attitudes than their nonengaged peers. Student engagement leads to positive student outcomes, improved academic achievement, and satisfaction, including higher standardized test scores and decreased dropout rates (Finley, 2014; Stephens, 2015).

Research has demonstrated that the more time a student spends engaged in classroom instruction, the more they learn. Students who are involved learn more efficiently, are more successful at remembering what they learn, and are more likely to be passionate about learning in general (Hurst, 2013). In contrast, the disengaged student will have lower cognitive performance and an increase in disruptive behaviors and pursue academic-avoidance behavior. Disengagement also exacerbates learning, behavior, and emotional problems and contributes to increased absenteeism and dropout rates (Finley, 2014).

The ability of a teacher to enjoy and have confidence in their teaching can play a vital role in students' motivation and engagement. Confidence and self-efficacy lends teachers the ability to propose alternative courses of action, enhance functioning through raised effort levels, and influence cognitive and emotional processes. As such, teachers are more likely to engage in pedagogy characterized by positive, proactive, and solution-focused orientations that results in increased student motivation and engagement (Stephens, 2015).

Students who believe teachers care about them believe they learn more (Finley, 2014; Stephens, 2015). Positive relationships with teachers can also lead to enhanced social, cognitive, and language development in younger children, as well as emotional, cognitive, and behavioral engagement in the classroom (Stephens, 2015). Teachers who are supportive of student autonomy facilitate greater motivation, curiosity, and a desire for challenge.

ACTIVE LEARNING

Engaging students in the learning process will increase attention and focus, motivate higher-level critical thinking, and promote meaningful learning experiences. Teachers who adopt a student-centered approach to their instructional methods will increase opportunities for student engagement and subsequently help students achieve the stated learning objectives (University of Washington, 2018).

Active learning requires students to participate in class instead of sitting quietly and paying attention. To engage students in the active learning process, teachers may wish to include brief question-and-answer sessions in their classroom instruction, as well as incorporate discussion into lectures, give impromptu writing assignments, and design hands-on activities and experiential learning events (University of Washington, 2018).

A student's curiosity and engagement with course content can be enhanced with great discussions that encourage student learning. While these types of discussions rarely happen spontaneously, advanced teacher preparation will help delineate a clear focus and set well-defined parameters to enable the class to address important topics from multiple perspectives (University of Washington, 2018).

STUDENT ROLES WITHIN THE CLASSROOM

The most important thing teachers can do to facilitate student engagement is to acknowledge their duty to help students learn. A student's ability to be engaged in his or her learning is essential, and learning through meaningful student involvement should include specific learning goals; meaningful action; and sustained, deep reflection (Fletcher, 2017).

As learners, students can play several roles within the classroom that can transform schools and education forever. Students may be facilitators, where knowledge comes from study, experience, and reflection. Engaging these students as guides will help reinforce their commitment to learning and the subject they are teaching to their peers. In addition to using students as guides, schools may want to hire students as paid staff members within the classroom and throughout the entire educational system (Fletcher, 2017).

As activity leaders and mentors, students can facilitate, teach, guide, direct, and otherwise lead youth, adults, and children in a plethora of ways. Mentoring is also a great way to establish nonhierarchical relationships between students and adults or among students themselves that will facilitate learning and guidance (Fletcher, 2017).

Students can also play the roles of decision maker and policy maker. In addition to making rules in the classroom, by participating in formal and informal decision making, students can be school board members and education committee members, among others. When students are provided the opportunity to research, plan, write, and evaluate educational rules, regulations, laws, and other policies, students as policy makers can enhance, validate, invigorate, and influence the outcomes of school policies in a variety of ways (Fletcher, 2017).

LEVELS OF STUDENT ENGAGEMENT

When a student is authentically engaged, they are immersed in work that has clear meaning and immediate value to them. Schoolwork that has little or no immediate meaning to students produces participation that is seen as ritual compliance and has such extrinsic outcomes as a passing grade. Students who see little or no meaning in their work and are, at best, merely passively complying with classroom requirements to avoid negative consequences, such as not having to stay in during recess to complete work, are clearly not engaged in the learning process (Hurst, 2013).

Students who are in a state of retreatism are disengaged from any assigned work and make no attempt to comply. Although these students are disengaged from the classroom, they are not disruptive to the learning of others. Those students in a rebellious level of engagement are disruptive, refuse to do the assigned work, and attempt to substitute alternative activities instead (Hurst, 2013).

While there are individual levels of student engagement, there are also engagement categories that can be used to measure the level of engagement for an entire classroom. An engaged classroom is where all students are authentically engaged at least some of the time or most of the students are authentically engaged most of the time. In these classrooms, passive compliance and retreatism are rarely observed, and rebellion is nonexistent. Compliant classrooms are what we consider to be engaged in the traditional form of education. They appear orderly, and most students seem to be working, yet retreatism very likely exists. In off-task classrooms, retreatism and rebellion exist, and some students are focused on authentic and ritual engagement, as well as passive compliance. Meanwhile, teachers spend most of their time dealing with rebelling students rather than teaching lessons that engage the students (Hurst, 2013).

TEACHING STRATEGIES AND CLASSROOM PRACTICES TO ENGAGE STUDENTS

Teachers must be familiar with the content of a lesson before teaching to ensure that their instruction and explanations are clear and concise. Processes for instruction should also be simple and predictable, following a familiar format that allows students to focus on the content instead of trying to navigate the instructional method and what is expected of them. To aid in efficient learning, teachers should explain the processes clearly and then check to see that the students understand by having them explain the processes and demonstrate expectations (Berrett, 2014).

To effectively engage students within their classroom, teachers should also demonstrate enthusiasm, preparedness, thoughtfulness, organization, and flexibility in their classroom presentations (BU Center for Teaching and Learning, 2018; Finley, 2014). Every time teachers show their excitement and enthusiasm about teaching, they leave positive impressions on students about the information being taught. Teachers should also purposely build frequent opportunities within the classroom for students to experience progress and success, be praised for their growth, and be encouraged to keep moving forward (Johnson, 2018).

For students to fully become engaged in the classroom, they will need to be challenged through academic rigor. Students should be given real-world questions and issues to solve through single activities, a collection of lessons, or an entire unit (Finley, 2014; McCarthy, 2015). Opportunities to apply concepts in practical ways are essential to learning, and having the opportunity to reflect on success and mistakes is essential to growth and innovation (McCarthy, 2015).

Deeper Learning

Teaching methods that favor lectures and rote learning appear to be standing in the way of making school relevant to more students. To make learning more relevant to students and therefore engage more students, schools should foster the concept of deeper learning. Deeper learning sets forth learning outcomes that include mastery of core academic content, critical thinking and problem solving, productive collaboration, effective communication, and the ability of students to direct their own learning and exhibit a strong academic mind-set (Martinez, 2014).

Deeper learning recognizes that teachers are only one source of knowledge, and students are highly encouraged to take responsibility for their own learning by pursuing their interests. Having responsibility for their own learning enables students the freedom to identify various resources beyond the classroom. Students can now use real-time virtual social media for multiple purposes. Students in an English class may talk with the authors of the books they read in class, or students in more technical courses can watch videos on design process (Martinez, 2014).

Practices that support student learning outcomes are necessary for engaging students, and research has shown that students who engage in deeper learning have better test scores, are more likely to enroll in four-year colleges, and report higher levels of academic engagement and motivation to learn (Martinez, 2014).

Positive Teacher–Student Relationships

High-quality teacher–student relationships are a crucial factor in determining student engagement, especially with challenging students and those from lower socioeconomic backgrounds (Pino-James, 2014). Close and caring relationships between teachers and students, where the teachers understand the students' perspectives, fulfill students' developmental need for connections with others and provide them a sense of belonging in society. Teachers can facilitate their relationships with students by caring about students' social and emotional needs, demonstrating knowledge of the students' lives, and increasing their one-on-one time with students (Finley, 2014; Pino-James, 2014). Teachers can display positive attitudes and enthusiasm while treating students fairly; however, it is imperative that deception and promise breaking are avoided (Pino-James, 2014).

Positive relationships are built when teachers provide affirmations to the student and let them know they are capable of doing well by using praise, written feedback, and other opportunities to recognize student success. Teachers show that they enjoy working with young students as individuals through humor while simultaneously facilitating student self-expression of ideas, values, and conceptions of self (Finley, 2014).

Relevancy, Meaningfulness, and Perception

To acquire a student's full engagement in school, teachers must create activities that engage high cognitive demands that students perceive as meaningful (Finley, 2014; Johnson, 2018; McCarthy, 2015; Pino-James, 2014). Through exploration, discovery, and application of their knowledge and skills to solve real-world problems, students are able to acquire new ideas and new knowledge that, in turn, develops mental pathways to long-term memory (Finley, 2014; Johnson, 2018).

Students who do not consider a learning activity worth their time and effort are unlikely to satisfactorily engage or may even disengage entirely (Pino-James, 2014). To ensure that activities are personally meaningful, teachers should connect skills and concepts to the students' interests, previous knowledge, and experiences, as well as highlight the value of the activity in relevant and meaningful ways (McCarthy, 2015; Pino-James, 2014).

Learning happens when concepts and practical applications are connected (McCarthy, 2015). Modeling may assist in making this connection by demonstrating why an individual activity is worth pursuing and when and how it is used in real life (Pino-James, 2014). To help students make an emotional connection to the themes and concepts being explored in class, teachers may want to launch the unit with an event that clearly outlines the outcomes of each lesson (McCarthy, 2015).

Students will pursue activities when they want to learn and understand rather than merely obtain a good grade, look smart, please their parents, or outperform their peers. To encourage this mastery orientation mind-set, teachers should consider various approaches, such as framing success in terms of learning rather than performing, emphasizing individual progress by reducing social comparisons, and recognizing student improvement and effort (Pino-James, 2014). Teachers should strive to provide feedback on a student's progress through questions, role-plays, or short quizzes, so that students will know how much they have accomplished and where more practice is needed (Johnson, 2018).

Competency

Research suggests that taking into account student behavior, cognition, and emotion when designing and implementing learning activities may help increase student engagement and thus positively affect student learning and achievement. A student's ability to effectively perform an activity, or their competence, can positively affect subsequent engagement. To help build a student's sense of competence in learning activities, teachers should create activities that are only slightly beyond the students' current levels of proficiency and where students can demonstrate their understanding throughout. Feedback loops should also be included to help students make progress in their work (Pino-James, 2014).

Autonomy

When a student's autonomy, or sense of control over behaviors and goals, is supported by a teacher's relinquishment of control, student engagement levels are likely to increase. A sense of autonomy can be implemented by consistently welcoming students' opinions and ideas into the classroom; using informational, noncontrolling language with students; and providing students time to understand and absorb an activity by themselves (Pino-James, 2014).

Classrooms that promote autonomy give students the space they need to make their own choices and take responsibility for their own learning. Autonomy can be encouraged by involving students in setting classroom norms and reflecting on their progress. Class meetings can be used as opportunities for students to solve problems for themselves, and taking on these responsibilities gradually enables students to see themselves as capable people who are constantly growing as learners (Boss, 2014).

Collaboration

Collaborative learning can also be an effective catalyst to student engagement. Research has demonstrated that working effectively with their peers can augment a student's level of engagement by creating a sense of connection during class activities (Pino-James, 2014). Collaborative learning involves group work, games, and projects that can be social and fun for students. Students are likely to become more engaged when the emphasis is on the construction of knowledge rather than the delivery of the content (Finley, 2014).

Group work can be made more productive when teachers employ strategies to ensure students know how to communicate and behave in the classroom. Modeling is an effective method that avoids uniform groups and grouping by ability and fosters individual accountability by assigning different roles that allow the teacher to effectively evaluate individual student and group performance (Pino-James, 2014).

Frequent and Effective Feedback

Positive feedback is essential in making sure students understand what they may have missed or did not understand from a lesson and how to change their learning strategies so that the same thing does not happen in future lessons. Teachers should advise students not to simply erase and replace their mistakes because they are unable to compare their work and will fail to understand where and why things went awry. Teachers should encourage students to first talk through what their mistakes were, logically reason out what they may need to do differently in the future, and then write the correct response next to the mistakes (Berrett, 2014).

All feedback should be positive, as negative feedback, including making students feel guilty or shamed over their mistakes, can be highly damaging to a student. Learning is in and of itself a process, not a destination. Students are likely to develop negative feelings and become disengaged from school based on experiences in which teachers shamed them for mistakes or lack of understanding and where the expectation was perfection instead (Berrett, 2014).

FROM BEGINNING TO END: CLASSROOM ACTIVITIES THAT FACILITATE STUDENT ENGAGEMENT

The heart of effective lesson planning to engage students exists in the beginnings and endings. If teachers fail to engage students at the start of a lesson by activating prior knowledge, creating anticipation, or establishing goals, student interest fades, and they may never become engaged. Likewise, when teachers fail to check for understanding and do not know if the lesson's goal was attained, they run the risk of moving carelessly from one activity to the next (Sztabnik, 2015).

Learning is a social and emotional experience, and achieving a sense of togetherness (or we) is crucial to establish before students can fully engage in classroom activities. Having this sense of "we" creates safety within the classroom and increases the likelihood that students will risk moving out of their comfort zones to try something new and ultimately learn (Foster, 2016). Building a safe classroom also allows teachers to connect with students who may feel alienated from school due to repeated failures, heavy-handed discipline, or negative stereotypes (Boss, 2014).

There are myriad strategies and classroom instructional practices that teachers should have in their tool box to engage students within the classroom (BU Center for Teaching and Learning, 2018). The following activities may be used to create a safe place where students will be engaged at the beginning and end of the day, as well as demonstrate an increase in sustained engagement throughout the day.

Attendance Questions

Teachers may wish to start each day using an open-ended question, such as "What is wrong with today?" or "What is the color of sadness?" while taking attendance. Questions should get the students thinking and spark interest in each other's responses. The beauty of this is that there are no right or wrong answers, and the questions are just enough outside the box to get students' attention and stretch their minds (Foster, 2016).

To demonstrate interest in the students, teachers may want to ask more personal questions, such as "What was the most interesting thing you saw on the way to school?" or "What was your favorite part of the summer?" (Foster, 2016). Questions of this nature help students see similarities and differences among their peers and allow them to feel a sense of togetherness when they discover they share common interests or see sadness the same way.

Good News

To create a safe space for students to take risks, teachers might start class with two minutes of sharing good news. Celebrating successes can build the comfort necessary for students to ask critical questions, share ideas, and participate in honest and open discussions (Sztabnik, 2015).

Talking in Class

Teachers may also want to spend the first few minutes of each class talking to their students, centering on their lives outside of the classroom. Topics can be sports, video games, movies, or anything else going on in the world. This personalized attention not only connects students with their peers, but it also makes them feel valued and treated as an individual rather than a body in a seat (Provenzano, 2016).

Increasing the Pace

It is a common misconception that teachers should go slow for students to really understand and become engaged in a lesson. Research demonstrates that, when instruction is at a stimulating pace, students have more opportunities to engage, respond, and move on to the next concept (Hurst, 2013).

Think-Pair-Share

In this strategy, teachers ask a question and then give students time to think about the answer quietly to themselves before pairing them up with another student or in small groups to discuss their ideas (BU Center for Teaching and Learning, 2018; Lemov, 2015). At the end of the day, students can also provide a three-minute summary of the key points of the day's class (BU Center for Teaching and Learning, 2018).

Debates

Debates are a fantastic way to spark interest and get students involved. Using case studies, students can analyze, make recommendations, and defend them. Teachers may wish to use the typical debate style by asking a question and having the students choose sides and defend their positions, or they can add a twist and organize students according to the side they want to argue but have them argue the opposite position. By arguing the opposite point of view, students are prompted to be more thoughtful about that point of view while becoming more thorough in defending their own (BU Center for Teaching and Learning, 2018).

Response Systems

Student response systems, such as clickers or raised hands, are another skillful way to get students engaged with what is happening in the classroom. Class votes can easily be taken to see what distinct positions students hold in class. Students may also be randomly called on using dice, a spinning wheel, or shuffled index cards containing their names to remove the perception that they are being picked on (BU Center for Teaching and Learning, 2018; Lemov, 2015).

YouTube

Reaching more 18- to 34-year-olds than any cable channel, YouTube contains hundreds of hours of video that provides something for every grade, subject, and approach. YouTube not only makes learning visible, but it also allows teachers to make connections to the real world that could never happen before (Sztabnik, 2015).

Across Disciplines

Integrating a variety of disciplines instructs students that ideas and concepts do not stand alone but exist within a greater knowledge base. Tossing a football around class before teaching the physics of a quarterback's spiral and measuring the angles of a Picasso painting in math class are just two ways that teachers can open a student's senses to deeper learning (Sztabnik, 2015).

10:2 Method and Think Time

For every 10 minutes of classroom instruction, teachers should allow students 2 minutes to process and respond to the instruction by writing what they have learned and questions they may have or by discussing the content with a classmate. Similarly, when teachers ask the class a question, students should be allowed five to seven seconds of thinking time before the teacher draws a random name to answer the question (Hurst, 2013).

Movement

Teachers can have students respond to questions by moving to a certain spot in the room, writing on whiteboards, or standing or sitting when they are done thinking about the question (Hurst, 2013).

Project-Based Learning

To help the least engaged student become highly engaged and encourage student voice and collaboration, teachers can use free-range project-based learning within the classroom, allowing students to choose the way in which they want to demonstrate their understanding of a concept or lesson (Larmer, Mergendoller, & Boss, 2015; Provenzano, 2016). Although teachers should provide rough guidelines of a rubric, students have the freedom to create their project, alter the rubric to meet the project, and then present it to the class. Students need to understand the material if they are going to create a project that demonstrates the needed skills, and they are more likely to become fully engaged in the lesson (Larmer et al., 2015). Student engagement is significantly increased when students take ownership of their projects (Provenzano, 2016).

For project-based learning to be successful, elevated expectations should be set for all students, and teachers should provide the necessary scaffolding to ensure that each student is working toward his or her full potential and mastery. Collaboration rather than competition should be encouraged so that students benefit from peer feedback and can help each other improve (Larmer et al., 2015).

Cultivating diversity is of utmost importance, and drawing on students' diverse backgrounds through music, literature, language, and current events to plan projects is imperative to successful student engagement. Students can also use this opportunity to share their thoughts and ideas, make decisions, and reflect on classroom experiences. Students need to feel that, not only is their class participation important, but also they as individuals are important and an asset to the classroom (Larmer et al., 2015).

Interest-Based Learning: Genius Hour/20 Time

To engage the most reluctant learners, a specific amount of time each day should be set aside that will give students the opportunity to explore something they are passionate about. This set time during class can be used for students to learn about their topics and share their information via blog posts, class updates, or even a virtual-style speech. This approach to student engagement and learning allows students to improve such skills as research, reading, writing, and speaking because they are doing something that matters to them (Provenzano, 2016; Wise Guys, 2017).

Jigsaw Classrooms

Jigsaw classrooms create points of contact between students who would otherwise not interact and allows students to see their classmates as authentic sources of knowledge. The fluid movement, flexible groupings, and redistribution of responsibility in these classrooms pushes students to be more actively engaged in what and how they learn (Hirsch, 2014).

To create a jigsaw classroom, teachers should divide lesson content into independent blocks and assign each piece to diverse groups of learners, strategically created to reflect differences in learning style, prior knowledge, or socioeconomic makeup. Each group then studies a different but complementary piece of the lesson, which allows students to master and possess unique knowledge of one piece of the lesson. Groups are then reshuffled into new groups consisting of one member, or expert, from each of the original groups, and each student is asked to share his or her individual knowledge, thus completing the puzzle, or lesson (Hirsch, 2014).

Engaging with Experts

Many parents, friends, and colleagues have expertise or know someone who can talk with, not to or at, the students during class time. Engaging in professional dialogue is an authentic practice that provides context for the subject-based skills, and the material and ideas are more likely to be embraced by students as they come from someone other than the teacher. Students are also more likely to become engaged in the material because the conversations with experts are give and take, enabling students to recognize themselves as contributors (McCarthy, 2015).

Personalizing Global Issues

When teachers include challenging topics, such as global warming, in their lesson plans, students should be given the opportunity to share personal reactions and responses to the material. Activities should allow students to engage in brainstorming, participate in working groups, and provide a productive outlet for the emotions that naturally rise to the surface. If certain topics cause students to become subdued or agitated, time should be allowed for open conversation, personal response, or reflective writing about their reactions to the lesson (Elias, 2013b).

Transition Circles

Teachers who find themselves working with transition students, for example moving from elementary to middle school or from middle school to high school, may want to use transition circles to discuss the challenges and rewards of transitioning to a new educational level. Students should be given the chance to speak on what they feel will be the challenges and opportunities, their concerns, and what they are most excited about. Index cards that can be shared in a community circle are a great alternative for students who wish to remain anonymous. Students can volunteer to read one of the cards and then open the discussion by asking other students to voluntarily comment on what is expressed on the card (Elias, 2013b). This format helps a new group of students get to know one another in a comfortable, nonthreatening way.

Self-Reflection Surveys

To fully engage students in their own learning, teachers can use age-appropriate learning goals and self-reflections that allow students to identify their current strengths and challenges as learners. Students may identify three each of (1) learning goals, (2) learning challenges, and (3) learning strengths. This socioemotional and academic learning approach allows students to create their own goals in each area for themselves and increases the likelihood they will engage in the classroom to meet them (Elias, 2013b).

Youth at Play

Play offers all the elements that engage a student's brain and keep mind and body healthy. It not only builds communication and social skills but play also teaches self-awareness and can be used to help build social and emotional learning skills (Ragsdale, 2014). When students are at play, they are connected to the world and actively engaged and present. In order to engage students and have them actively present in the classroom, teachers may want to incorporate strategies involving play.

Teachers may begin with a name game or ice breaker to help students get to know everyone in the classroom and create a sense of family. Name games not only allow students to bond quickly, feel accepted, and create a sense of cultural pride, but they also allow the students eventually to feel safe within the classroom. Students can also get to know each other better by pairing up for five minutes and teaching their partners something they know how to do or sharing information they may know about the class subject. Teachers can then call on volunteers to demonstrate what they learned from their partners (Ragsdale, 2014).

Games can also be used to establish classroom norms and rules. Students can be placed in groups based on their favorite sports and asked to pick one rule from the sport that they feel is the most important and the consequence for breaking that rule. Once a collective list is made, students can then translate the list in terms of class rules and how they want to work and play together (Ragsdale, 2014). The list should include what the students need from themselves and from each other in order to learn effectively, and it should be stated in positive language (Elias, 2013a).

Level Up

Students love to play video games because of the constant reward for reaching new levels and earning higher rankings, which creates a sense of accomplishment, competency, and worth. Teachers can engage this need in the classroom by developing levels of proficiency based on set standards. At the end of a lesson, students should have the ability to chart their own progress toward mastery based on those standards, and this may be just the right motivation to engage reluctant learners (Sztabnik, 2015).

3-2-1 Method

The 3-2-1 method of summarizing is commonly used at the end of a lesson and has students record three things they learned, two things they found interesting, and one question they still have about the lesson. Adequate time should be allowed for students to share their findings with a classmate (Hurst, 2013).

Exit Tickets

Exit tickets are a quick and comprehensive way to collect formative assessment data and instructional strategy feedback while providing students with methods of self-analysis and open communication (Sztabnik, 2015).

Notes of Influence

To end class with a positive climate, notes of influence can be written by students stating one thing they learned from someone else in class. These notes can then be stuck to the chalkboard and read aloud at the beginning of the next day to reaffirm that the classroom is a community of learners. This method validates student participation and helps students understand at a deeper level of learning (Szabnik, 2015).

FINAL THOUGHTS

Student engagement involves not only behavioral activity within a classroom but also emotional and cognitive involvement in academic activities. Students who are fully and authentically engaged in their education will display increased effort, improved academic achievement, and more positive student learning outcomes. The more time students spend engaged in learning, the more passionate they are about learning, the more efficient they are at learning, and the more they remember what they learn—they just learn more, period.

When students are authentically engaged in their education, they are immersed in work that has clear meaning and immediate value to them. It is essential to student growth and innovation that students are provided opportunities to apply concepts in practical ways and have the occasion to reflect on their success and mistakes. To acquire a student's full engagement in school, it is essential that teachers create activities that students perceive as meaningful by connecting skills and concepts to the students' interests, previous knowledge, and experiences, as well as highlight the value of the activity in relevant and meaningful ways.

POINTS TO REMEMBER

- Learning is in and of itself a process, not a destination. The most important thing teachers can do to facilitate student engagement is to acknowledge their duty to help students learn.
- A teacher's ability to enjoy his or her work; his or her confidence level; and positive, proactive, and solution-focused pedagogy all result in increased student motivation and engagement. To effectively engage students, teachers should be enthusiastic, prepared, thoughtful, organized, and flexible.
- Engaging students in the learning process increases attention and focus, motivates higher-level critical thinking skills, and promotes meaningful learning experiences.
- Student engagement can be at an individual level (authentic, ritual compliance, retreatism, rebellion), as well as the classroom level (engaged, compliant, off task).

Chapter Six

Ensuring That All Students Receive Support

A Spotlight on Special Education, At-Risk, and ELL Programs

Students with disabilities can have school experiences that are positively or negatively influenced by the attitudes and behaviors of their peers, administrators and staff, and school policies. Although the Americans with Disabilities Act of 1990 protects the inherent rights of individuals with disabilities, it cannot always protect students from subtle forms of discrimination and prejudice (Milsom, 2017). Administrators, teachers, and counselors can help to create a more positive school experience that promotes the academic, career, and personal and social growth of students with disabilities.

Research shows that children without disabilities generally prefer to interact with children without either physical or intellectual disabilities. Teachers were shown to have more negative attitudes toward students with behavioral and emotional problems than toward those with disabilities, as the former group of students had a stronger negative impact on the school and its students (Milsom, 2017).

Negative attitudes do not always translate into negative behavior, yet they have been linked to bias and discrimination. In fact, research has shown that teachers who have negative attitudes toward students with disabilities expect lower achievement and more inappropriate behavior than they do from students without disabilities. Students with disabilities may not have as many opportunities as their peers if the school's principal possesses a negative attitude and discourages, or even prevents, them from completing the regular academic coursework necessary to enter higher education (Milsom, 2017).

The negative attitudes and actions of educators and peers can be internalized by students with disabilities and lead to a negative effect on their behavior. Students with disabilities are strongly influenced by the attitudes and expectations of others, and negative effects may emerge in their social relationships, education, employment, and health (Milsom, 2017).

Recently, students with disabilities have reported feeling disrespected and misunderstood by teachers and peers. They have stated that teachers did not notice derogatory comments directed at them by their classmates and thus believed teachers did not care about them. As a result, students with disabilities felt alienated, disinterested, and anxious about their classroom, teachers, and classmates (Milsom, 2017).

Research suggests that teachers and administrators may hold negative attitudes toward students with disabilities because they did not receive adequate training on how to work with students with disabilities and subsequently felt unprepared to provide effective services to them. Teachers report feeling stressed when working with a student with a disability because they felt incompetent and unknowledgeable about inclusive education for all students (Mader, 2017).

With the passage of disability legislation and the Every Student Succeeds Act of 2015, schools are now more accountable for student outcomes. As a result, administrators are placing additional demands on themselves and teachers, creating high levels of stress, and they worry that one group of students will suffer for another (Klein, 2016; Samuels, 2016).

For these reasons, professional development activities are essential to creating positive school experiences for students with disabilities (Mizell, 2010). Professional training also increases awareness about students with disabilities for regular education teachers who may not be as well versed, as well as serves as an additional resource for special education teachers (McLeskey, 2011). Trainings can center on one specific content area, such as behavioral interventions for students with disabilities, or focus on the promotion of cooperative relationships between students with disabilities and students without disabilities (Blanton, Pugach, & Florian, 2014).

Professional development activities can also help teachers address the needs of all learners by teaching them how to design and modify their class lessons so that they will benefit a range of learning styles (Milsom, 2017).

Learning creative methods of instruction and assessment assists teachers in reframing their approaches to teaching and learning and leads to less frustration and stress related to accommodating students with disabilities (McLeskey, 2011; Milsom, 2017).

Positive contact with students with disabilities is one of the most effective ways to help students gain an understanding of and knowledge about students with disabilities. Social interactions between students with and without disabilities, such as cooperative learning groups, can provide both social and academic benefits to students with disabilities. Collaborative problem solving can provide students without disabilities a voice to raise concerns related to students' disabilities and help them develop understanding and empathy (Milsom, 2017).

Through cooperative interactions, students benefit by gaining an appreciation for diversity in general. Schools that teach empathy and promote respect for others through the general curriculum can help students develop tolerance and respect for differences. Character education programs can also be used as a base from which discussions and activities specific to students with disabilities can be integrated into the classroom (Milsom, 2017).

CREATIVE WAYS TO ENGAGE SPECIAL EDUCATION STUDENTS

Interacting with special education students requires flexibility and creativity and can be a rewarding experience. To engage students with disabilities in the classroom, teachers must learn the individual needs and interests of each student and transform them into such classroom activities as the following to help them grow and thrive (Saint Joseph's University, 2018).

Question Formulation Technique

This technique does more than simply have teachers teach students. Instead, students are prompted to ask all kinds of questions about any subject; for example, when teaching about art, teachers can provide a painting or sculpture and answer questions the students ask about the piece of art (Saint Joseph's University, 2018).

Musical Instruction and Lessons

Music is a powerful tool and can be used to engage students with a wide range of disabilities and learning disorders. Research has shown that rhythm and melody help improve memory and the understanding of key words, and by turning instructions and lessons into songs, students are more likely to learn and retain key information (Spray, 2015). Students will also be more engaged in the lesson if they are able to sing and drum along with the music (Saint Joseph's University, 2018).

Menu Options

Student engagement is heightened when classroom lessons and information are connected to real-world activities. Anything from outside the classroom may be brought into the classroom and connected to a learning activity. For instance, bringing a menu from the outside world into the classroom and having students select questions to answer from categories labeled "Appetizer," "Entrée," and "Dessert" is a great way to engage students (Saint Joseph's University, 2018).

Student Creations

Strategies to help students create something varies, as the goal is to work with, and within, each student's individual capabilities to stimulate creativity. Having students with disabilities create something not only promotes student engagement, but it also helps increase student confidence (Saint Joseph's University, 2018).

INSTRUCTIONAL PROCESSES THAT PROMOTE STUDENT ENGAGEMENT

Students with learning disabilities can become frustrated when they see themselves as incompetent in school and subsequently become unmotivated and unexcited to read, write, and complete assignments for fear of failure, embarrassment, and disrespect. When a student's competence improves, motivation also increases, generating a cycle of engagement, motivation, and competence that supports enhanced academic achievement (Weiser, 2014).

Giving students with disabilities a choice in what they are going to do, whether it be in writing, math, or reading, is one of the greatest motivators. Having choices allows all students to take a more active role in their learning and holds them accountable for finishing assignments and activities. When students choose their own activities or assignments, they are more likely to take charge of what they are doing and will generally be more successful at the task (Weiser, 2014). When students have a choice of what they read, they become more engaged in what they are reading and read for a longer period of time (Wood, 2016).

Differentiation

Differentiation is a teaching process that can be used for students of differing abilities in an inclusion classroom or a self-contained resource room and has numerous benefits for students with disabilities, including the maximization of each student's growth and individual learning needs. Using this approach, differentiated assignments are combined with student choice, empowering students with disabilities to be in control of their options, and teachers direct the learning process that will best meet the students' readiness, interests, and learning styles (Mastropieri & Scruggs, 2018).

Choice boards contain lists of teacher-designed activities that best meet the specific needs of each student and are directly aligned to learning goals and skills. These boards should be placed in student folders, in centers, on bulletin boards, or on handouts and can be used to reinforce, practice, or enhance content knowledge and academic objectives. Students are then able to make a choice from a particular group of assignments, and the teacher targets work toward that student's needs (Weiser, 2014).

RAFT

Instead of writing traditional essays to explain or summarize concepts, the RAFT strategy encourages creative thinking, different points of view, alternate opinions, and recall of content knowledge to enhance students' understanding of narratives and expository text. Through this strategy, content can be differentiated for students with various academic skills and knowledge levels (Weiser, 2014).

To engage in this process, students assume a role (R) as a specific type of writer, such as teacher, reporter, or observer. Once chosen, students consider who their audience (A) is, to whom are they writing and who will be reading. Next, students decide what format (F) they will complete the writing in. It could be in the form of a letter, newspaper article, or e-mail. Last, a topic (T) should be determined and the subject of the research chosen. Students might choose to write about an athlete, a mountain range, or even a chemistry term (Weiser, 2014).

By using RAFT, students with disabilities are able to enhance their higher-level thinking skills and reflect on what they have read. Instead of just writing answers, students process information to complete the writing assignment (Weiser, 2014). Most importantly, this strategy gives students a choice in how they express what they have learned.

Verb Change

Another way to empower and engage students with learning disabilities is to give them a choice in their assignments to either learn or review a concept, event, or text content by changing the verb in the activity or question (Weiser, 2014). Instead of asking students to "write" about the life of George Washington, for example, teachers can ask students to "interview" George Washington or ask students to "imagine" they are George Washington and tell his grandchildren about his greatest achievements. During reading and language arts, instead of checking for understanding by writing down three events that happened in a chapter of *Charlotte's Web*, engage students by asking them to draw three events that happened in the chapter.

STRATEGIES TO SUPPORT STUDENTS WITH IEPS IN GENERAL AND INCLUSION CLASSROOMS

According to students, they are more likely to be involved with learning when presented opportunities to be creative and involved with their peers. Students also feel they learn more from discussions, debates, art, drama, and technology projects. To foster a learning environment that supports student engagement, teachers should encourage and support a student's curiosity, need for understanding, originality, and creativity. Teachers should also strive to build and support meaningful, reciprocal, and respectful relationships by acknowledging a student's need for involvement with others (Thompson, 2015).

By supporting and strengthening engagement, teachers help students with disabilities build their self-esteem. To do this, educators must clearly articulate the criteria that students must meet for success and provide clear, immediate, and constructive feedback. Educators should never assume that certain skills are already mastered by the student; it is better to model all skills and problem-solving techniques for student success (Thompson, 2015).

Universal Design

The highest encompassing approach to student engagement for all students, not just students with disabilities, is the use of Universal Design for Learning (UDL) principles. Through UDL, teachers can provide multiple ways for students to acquire information and knowledge; alternatives for demonstrating knowledge; and a variety of ways to tap into student interests, increase motivation, and incorporate challenges (CAST, 2018).

To gain student interest in classroom activities and assignments, teachers should optimize individual student choice, relevance, value, and authenticity while minimizing any threats and distractions. To sustain a high level of student effort and persistence, teachers should highlight the importance of goals and objectives, vary demands and resources to optimize challenge, foster collaboration and community, and increase the amount of feedback students receive. Educators should provide options for student self-regulation by promoting expectations and beliefs that optimize motivation, facilitate personal coping skills and strategies, and develop self-assessment and reflection activities (Thompson, 2015).

Whole-Group Response

Students with learning disabilities are often taught in whole-group instruction instead of differentiated small-group instruction in inclusive classrooms. This style of instruction becomes problematic when teachers try to actively engage all students; however, there are strategies that can be used to accommodate a wide range of individual student needs (Nagro, Hooks, Fraser, & Cornelius, 2016).

To successfully include students with disabilities into general education settings, teachers must foster a sense of belonging and strive to incorporate strategies that increase active participation, peer interaction, and self-evaluation (Nagro et al., 2016). There is a continuum of strategies that allows teachers to maintain student engagement and monitor student progress during whole-group instruction.

Hand Signals

One strategy that teachers may employ to promote student engagement and check for comprehension is the use of hand signals, particularly for class discussions; for example, during class discussions, teachers may have students who want to share new ideas hold up one finger and students who want to add to the current idea hold up two fingers (Cowen & Nee, 2016). In this manner, teachers can prevent discussions from veering off topic and ensure a comprehensive discussion of the topic before moving on to another (Nagro et al., 2016).

Conducting conversations by using hand signals also increases comprehension and targets both cognitive and metacognitive development, while holding students accountable for their learning by asking them to self-evaluate and reengage in the learning process (Cowen & Nee, 2016; Nagro et al., 2016). Teachers are also able to redirect discussions and lessons before students become frustrated and disengaged.

Peer-to-Peer Discourse

Peer discussion opportunities that are based on the student's degree of understanding are a great way for students with disabilities to engage in peer learning. Students who feel confident enough to teach their classmates can pair up with those who are not sure if they understand the material. In this way, students with disabilities can listen to their classmates use age-appropriate language that emphasizes the concepts and self-correct their own thinking. At the same time, teachers can measure the level of student learning and understanding of concepts by listening to conversations and making assessments (Nagro et al., 2016).

Choral Responses

Whole-group responding, in which questions are posed to the entire class and require students to answer verbally in unison, makes it difficult for teachers to track individual student accuracy, enabling students with disabilities to become passive learners. To increase student participation, teachers should use response cards. This method requires students to hold up cards with predetermined answers to respond to a teacher-initiated stimulus, thus eliminating the need for verbal responses (Nagro et al., 2016).

Response cards can also be used for students with learning disabilities who struggle with writing mechanics, such as handwriting, spelling, vocabulary, and text structure. Cards can be designed as true and false; multiple choice; or more content specific, such as a set of vocabulary words, parts of speech, or story elements. For those students who struggle with organizational skills and making connections, key words to a multistep problem can be written on the response cards to further monitor comprehension and sustain student attention and engagement (Nagro et al., 2016).

Other Whole-Group Strategies

Other whole-group response strategies include written responses on exit tickets, open-ended poll questions, surveys, and dry-erase boards. In certain situations, particularly those in which teachers need to accurately capture and make judgments about student learning, written responses may be more appropriate than hand signals or response cards. For instance, the use of dry-erase boards allows students to write a vocabulary term, rewrite a sentence using correct punctuation, or create pictorial or figurative written responses and provides the teacher with immediate feedback (Nagro et al., 2016).

STUDENTS WHO ARE AT RISK

Health and Nutrition

Students from low-income families are less likely to get proper diagnoses, receive appropriate health care, or obtain appropriate medications and interventions. They also have more hearing loss issues due to untreated ear infections, greater exposure to lead, and a higher incidence of asthma than middle-class children. Studies have linked intelligence to health, and each of these health-related factors can affect attention, reasoning, learning, and memory (Jensen, 2013).

Nutrition also plays a crucial role, and students who grow up in low-income families are exposed to food with lower nutritional value, which can then in turn affect gray matter mass in their brains (Jensen, 2013). Skipping breakfast is widespread with urban minority students and negatively affects their academic achievement, cognition, and attendance (Stuber, 2014).

When students are faced with both poor nutrition and diminished health practices, it becomes harder for them to listen, concentrate, and learn. Lead exposure can lead to poor working memory and a weaker ability to link cause and effect. Students with numerous untreated ear infections can have trouble with sound discrimination and subsequently have a hard time following directions, completing highly demanding auditory processing, and understanding the teacher (Jensen, 2013). In addition to these diminished academic skills, poor nutrition can affect behavior, leaving students with visibly low energy or hyperactivity from a sugar high (Jensen, 2013; Stuber, 2014).

Teachers should never withhold recess or physical education from students for disciplinary reasons, as they both contribute to greater oxygen intake and better learning. Physical education programs allow students to perform at their highest level academically. The use of games, movement, and drama triggers the release of glucose, and proper levels of glucose have been associated with stronger memory and cognitive function (Jensen, 2013; Stuber, 2014). In essence, exercise and physical activity can reduce some of the issues linked to poor nutrition and will build student health.

Vocabulary

Research has demonstrated that students who grow up in low socioeconomic conditions typically have a smaller vocabulary than middle-class children, raising the risk for academic failure (Colker, 2014; Jensen, 2013). Statistics show that students from low-income families hear an average of 13 million words by age four; middle-class students, 26 million words; and upper-income students, 46 million words (Jensen, 2013). This sets the average disparity at 30 million words for four-year-olds (Colker 2014).

The brain uses vocabulary as a tool for learning, memory, and cognition, and words help students represent, manipulate, and reframe information. Students from low-income families are less likely to know the words a teacher uses in class or the words that appear in reading material than students from other socioeconomic brackets. When students are unfamiliar with the vocabulary used in school, they do not read, tune out, do not participate in class, and feel they do not belong in school (Jensen, 2013).

Building a student's vocabulary is essential and should be a key part in student engagement experiences. Teachers can have students create trading cards, where students write a vocabulary word on one side of an index card and a sentence using the word correctly on the other side. Students can also do a class mixer and test other students by giving a new word to a partner and then have the partner use the word in a sentence. Alternatively, teachers can draw cards from a bowl and ask students to use the word in a sentence orally or have them write a sentence on a white board (Jensen, 2013).

Effort

Teachers who are unfamiliar with the difficulties low-income families face may think that students from those families are lazy because they slouch, slump, and show little effort in class, when in fact these students are unmotivated due to lack of hope and optimism. Students who show little or no effort are actually giving teachers feedback about themselves and the class they are in. When students like their class, they work harder; when they are excited, curious, and intrigued, they put forth more effort (Jensen, 2013).

Student engagement is central to keeping students in school. To engage students and strengthen relationships with them, teachers should reveal more about themselves and learn more about their students. Learning should be the student's idea, and teachers should offer choices and involve students in decision making. Class activities and information should be connected and relevant to the students' real world, and students should not only have choices in what they want to do and how to do it, but they also should be the ultimate decision maker (Jensen, 2013).

Teachers should aim to provide effective feedback and support and encourage students' efforts on a daily basis. Student learning and growth is optimized when teachers give more positives than negatives, and when students are challenged and encouraged and their efforts upheld, they will work harder and become more engaged (Jensen, 2013).

Research suggests that students from low socioeconomic backgrounds see negative events in their world and in their future. Having little or no expectation of positive future events can lead to a sense of hopelessness that bleeds into their expectations of learning and achievements at school (Jensen, 2013). Lack of hope and a student's predetermined mind-set that he or she is not smart can be a significant liability (Brock & Hundley, 2016; Dweck, 2007). In turn, hope and a student's belief that he or she is smart or can become smarter are significant assets. When students think they will fail, they are unlikely to try, and if they believe they are not smart and cannot succeed, they will not put forth any effort (Dweck, 2007; Jensen, 2013). Conversely, when students believe they are smart and will succeed, they will try and put forth their best effort (Brock & Hundley, 2016; Dweck, 2007).

When students believe that they have a predetermined and set amount of intelligence that will never change, student engagement and learning are influenced. Teachers should make it clear to students through positive feedback that brains do change and grow, including theirs (Brock & Hundley, 2016). Phrases that suggest a student is not good enough at something and has other strengths should be avoided; rather, effort should be made to affirm and reinforce the student's level of effort, guide him or her in making smarter choices and developing a positive attitude (Brock & Hundley, 2016; Jensen, 2013).

Students from low-income families typically show cognitive deficits, such as short attention spans, high levels of distractibility, difficulty examining the value of their work, and struggling with forming new solutions to problems. Many of these students struggle cognitively and begin to exhibit problem behavior or shut down and display learned helplessness. Students who struggle with reading, math, and simply following directions often have weak vocabulary, poor working memory, or poor processing skills. Cognitive capacity is teachable, and teachers can help underperforming students by including core cognitive skills as part of their lessons (Jensen, 2013).

Stress and Distress

Acute and chronic stress, or distress, is toxic to students. Living in poverty creates chronic stress for parents, which in turn affects their students through the activation of their immune systems and subsequently strains a student's available resources. Distress affects brain development, academic success, and social competence, as well as impairs behavior and working memory, reduces attentional control, and boosts impulsivity (Jensen, 2013). As a result, distressed students can exhibit one of two behaviors: angry, "in your face" assertiveness or disconnected, "leave me alone" passivity. These students may appear to be out of control or lazy or have an attitude, yet their symptoms replicate those of stress disorders that influence student engagement. Aggressive behaviors can take the form of talking back to the teacher, using inappropriate body language, and making inappropriate facial expressions, while the more passive behaviors include failing to respond to questions or requests, exhibiting passivity, slumping or slouching, and disconnecting from peers or academic work (Jensen, 2013).

If teachers address the underlying and real issue of distress, symptoms will diminish over time. Building stronger relationships with students helps alleviate student stress and gives students a person to trust and who believes in them. Embedding more fun into academic activities and allowing students to choose what this looks like not only reduces stress but also provides students more control over their own lives while at school (Jensen, 2013). Providing students with choices and allowing them to participate in class decision making also encourages responsibility and leadership.

To better deal with stressors, students should be taught coping skills that they can use in and out of the classroom; for example, teachers can give students a simple "If this, then that" strategy for solving problems with new skills. Teachers can tell stories about their own daily stressors, allow students to brainstorm solutions, and then share and model the coping mechanisms that worked (Jensen, 2013).

ENGLISH LANGUAGE LEARNERS

There are many ways to support and engage English language learners (ELLs), even if they are at the beginning levels of English proficiency. There are a variety of ideas that can make content more accessible, strengthen language development, and provide students with the opportunity to fully participate in class instruction and activities (Colorín Colorado, 2017).

Background Knowledge

To prepare lessons involving ELLs, teachers should first determine what background knowledge students need in order to master the material. ELLs' background knowledge can vary significantly from one student to another, and it is important for teachers not to assume that all background knowledge matches for students from the same country (Colorín Colorado, 2017; Robertson, 2014). For example, students may not have studied geography in their previous educational experiences, and the concepts of a city, state, or country may be new and confusing. Teachers should also keep in mind different cultural backgrounds. For example, some countries teach students that there are only five or six continents instead of seven (Colorín Colorado, 2017).

In order to build background knowledge, teachers should create interest in the subject by designing class materials using pictures, real objects, maps, or personal experiences that are relevant to students' lives (Colorín Colorado, 2017; Fishtree, 2017; Robertson, 2014). Text-specific knowledge should be provided to students beforehand, particularly when the concepts are difficult or there is a plethora of information. Concept backgrounds can also be developed by explaining difficult concepts and assigning key words; for example, the teacher might say, "This is the Statue of Liberty. *Liberty* means 'freedom.' *Liberty* means *libertad*. The people of France gave us the Statue of Liberty" (Colorín Colorado, 2017).

Cooperative Learning

Cooperative learning not only is a powerful way to help students learn and master content material, but it also provides the opportunity for students to work together within the classroom. Cooperative learning also opens up opportunities for students to practice vocabulary and to be supported by their peers during the process (Colorín Colorado, 2017; Fishtree, 2017). For reading, ELLs can be assigned a reading partner who is friendly and fluent in reading. Partners can read aloud to each other, alternating sentences or pages, and then summarize what they have read.

Another reading strategy is Think-Pair-Share, a collaborative learning strategy where students work together to solve a problem or answer a question about an assigned reading (Lemov, 2015). With this method, students must think independently about a topic or answer to a question and then share their ideas with classmates. Discussing the answer with a partner helps to increase student contributions, concentrate attention, and engage students in comprehending the reading material (Colorín Colorado, 2017).

ELLs can also demonstrate their understanding of class content through the writing process. Student teams can compose questions about subject material, and teachers can then use those questions on an exam. Alternatively, students can write a short and simple synopsis of what they have read (Colorín Colorado, 2017).

Repetition

Repetition is essential to helping students learn and retain new words or concepts, and where possible, teachers should combine multiple methods to teach the same vocabulary. Combining text, audio, and visual media enables ELLs to easily recognize and master new words; for example, bingo is an effective and versatile game that teachers can use for younger learners, while teachers of older students can have them think of words related to weather and create a mind map of related terms (Fishtree, 2017).

Parental Involvement

No matter the language, parental support is an enormous factor in a student's academic success. ELL families are often at a disadvantage in supporting their student due to language and cultural barriers, and teachers can interpret this difficulty as a lack of interest in education. In reality, ELL parents want their students to succeed but are unable to participate to the same extent as other parents (Mapp & Kuttner, 2013; Robertson, 2014).

Consistent, open, and friendly communication from teachers can make a significant impact on ELL parent participation (Grant & Ray, 2016). With the help of an ELL family member or a bilingual school staff member, teachers can communicate positive information about the students, enabling parents to feel more comfortable asking questions and visiting the school in the future. The more armed parents are with the information necessary to help their students be successful, the more likely their students will receive support at home (Robertson, 2014).

FINAL THOUGHTS

School experiences of students with disabilities can be positively or negatively influenced by the attitudes and behaviors of their peers, teachers, and general school policies. The Americans with Disabilities Act of 1990 protects the inherent rights of individuals with disabilities but does not necessarily protect students from discrimination and prejudice. School administrators and teachers can create a more positive school experience that promotes the academic, career, and personal and social growth of students with disabilities.

Students with disabilities can be influenced by the attitudes and expectations of others, and negative effects emerge in their social relationships, education, employment, and health as a result. Students with disabilities report feeling disrespected, misunderstood, and uncared about, resulting in feelings of alienation, disinterest, and anxiety. To make students feel connected and be more engaged, teachers need to learn the individual needs and interests of each student and transform them into classroom activities. Teachers should also encourage and support a student's curiosity, need for understanding, originality, and creativity and strive to build and support meaningful, reciprocal, and respectful relationships.

Student engagement is central to keeping students in school, and to fully engage students, teachers need to strengthen their relationships with them. Learning should be the students' idea, and they should be presented with choices and opportunities for decision making. Class activities and information should be connected and relevant to the students' real world so that they can make sense of and apply the learned knowledge outside the classroom.

POINTS TO REMEMBER

- Professional development activities are essential to creating positive school experiences for students with disabilities. Professional training increases awareness about students with disabilities, helps teachers address the needs of all learners, and instructs teachers on redesigning and modifying classroom instruction.

- Giving students with disabilities a choice in what they are going to do is one of the greatest motivators. Having choices allows all students to take a more active role in their learning and take ownership of their learning and holds them more accountable for achieving their goals.
- Although student engagement is heightened when educational lessons and activities are connected to the student's perception of the real world, the highest encompassing approach to student engagement for all students is the use of Universal Design for Learning (UDL) principles (CAST, 2018). When using UDL, teachers provide multiple ways for students to learn, demonstrate their knowledge, tap into their own interests, be more motivated, and rise to challenges.

References

Alber, R. (2014). 5 ways to give your students more voice and choice. *Edutopia*. Retrieved from https://www.edutopia.org/blog/five-strategies-more-voice-choice-students-rebecca-alber.

Allen, J. (2016). *Becoming a literacy leader*. Portland, ME: Stenhouse.

Altobello, N., & Shapiro, D. (2017). *Mentoring: At the crossroads of education, business and community: The power and promise of private sector engagement in youth mentoring*. Retrieved from https://www.mentoring.org/new-site/wp-content/uploads/2015/09/EY_Full_Report-1.pdf.

Alvermann, D. E. (2002). *Adolescents and literacies in a digital world*. New York: Peter Lang.

Ambler, G. (2013). How leadership gurus define leadership. Retrieved from http://www.georgeambler.com/defining-leadership/.

Anderson, C. (2017). Youth mentoring: 5 steps to starting a program at your business. *Groupon Merchant Blog*. Retrieved from https://www.groupon.com/merchant/blog/5-steps-starting-youth-mentoring-program-business.

Anderson, L. W., & Krathwohl, D. R. (2001). *A taxonomy for learning, teaching, and assessing* (Abridged ed.). Boston: Allyn & Bacon.

Baigelman, L. (2014). Ten ways to encourage your middle-schooler to read. Retrieved from http://torcschools.tcms.schooldesk.net/Portals/Torcschools/Tcms/docs/10%20Ways%20to%20Encourage%20Your%20Middle-Schooler%20to%20Read%20-%20Understood.pdf.

Balcazar, F. E., & Keys, C. B. (2014). Goals in mentoring relationships. In D. L. DuBois & M. J. Karcher (Eds.), *Handbook of youth mentoring* (2nd ed., pp. 83–98). Thousand Oaks, CA: Sage.

Barron, B., & Darling-Hammond, L. (2008). Teaching for meaningful learning: A review of research on inquiry-based and cooperative learning. *Edutopia*. Retrieved from https://backend.edutopia.org/sites/default/files/pdfs/edutopia-teaching-for-meaningful-learning.pdf.

Bashi, V. (1991). Mentoring of at-risk students. Retrieved from https://www.irp.wisc.edu/publications/focus/pdfs/foc132d.pdf.

References

Beers, K. (2005). Choosing not to read: Understanding why some middle schoolers just say no. Retrieved from http://www.csun.edu/~krowlands/Content/Academic_Resources/Reading/Useful%20Articles/Beers-Choosing%20not%20to%20Read.pdf.

Belotti, C. L. (2016). Cross-age peer mentoring to improve sixth-grade student reading (Doctoral dissertation, Walden University, 2016). Retrieved from http://scholarworks.waldenu.edu/cgi/viewcontent.cgi?article=3890&context=dissertations.

Belt, L. (2015). One child at a time: The case of school-based mentoring. *American Institutes for Research*. Retrieved from http://www.sedl.org/pubs/sedletter/v14n01/.

Bergland, C. (2014). Tackling the "vocabulary gap" between rich and poor children. *Psychology Today*. Retrieved from https://www.psychologytoday.com/blog/the-athletes-way/201402/tackling-the-vocabulary-gap-between-rich-and-poor-children.

Berrett, S. (2014). The 4 C's of effective instruction that boost student engagement. *Reading Horizons*. Retrieved from https://www.readinghorizons.com/blog/effective-instruction-that-boost-student-engagement.

Black, D. S., Grenard, J. L., Sussman, S., & Rohrbach, L. A. (2010). The influence of school-based natural mentoring relationships on school attachment and subsequent adolescent risk behaviors. *Health Education Research, 25*(5), 892–902. doi:10.1093/her/cyq040.

Blad, E. (2017). To fill a "mentoring gap," schools gets creative. *Education Week*. Retrieved from https://www.edweek.org/ew/articles/2017/10/18/to-fill-a-mentoring-gap-schools-get.html.

Blanton, L. P., Pugach, M., & Florian, L. (2014). Preparing general education teachers to improve outcomes for students with disabilities. Retrieved from https://www.ncld.org/wp-content/uploads/2014/11/aacte_ncld_recommendation.pdf.

Blow, M. (2011). Motivating middle school students. *Scholastic*. Retrieved from http://www.scholastic.com/teachers/classroom-solutions/2011/04/motivating-middle-school-students?pImages=n&x=50&y=8.

Boss, S. (2014). Creating a welcoming and intellectually challenging classroom. *Edutopia*. Retrieved from https://www.edutopia.org/blog/creating-welcoming-and-intellectually-challenging-classroom-suzie-boss.

Bradshaw Foundation. (2011). The cave paintings of the Lascaux Cave. Retrieved from http://www.bradshawfoundation.com/lascaux/.

Britner, P. A., Blacazar, F. E., Blechman, E. A., Blinn-Pike, L., & Larose, S. (2006). Mentoring special youth populations. *Journal of Community Psychology, 34*(6), 747–763. DOI: 10.1002/jcop.20127.

Bray, B. (2012). 10 steps to encourage student voice and choice. Retrieved from https://barbarabray.net/2012/02/03/10-steps-to-encourage-student-voice-and-choice/.

Brock, A., & Hundley, H. (2016). *The growth mindset coach: A teacher's month-by-month handbook for empowering students to achieve*. Berkeley, CA: Ulysses Press.

Bronk, K. C. (2011). The role of purpose in life in healthy identity formation: A grounded model. *New Directions for Student Leadership, 132*, 31–44.

Brown, D. F., & Knowles, T. (2007). *What every middle school teacher should know*. Portsmouth, NH: Heinemann.

Bruce, M., & Bridgeland, J. (2014). The mentoring effect: Young people's perspectives on the outcomes and availability of mentoring. Retrieved from https://files.eric.ed.gov/fulltext/ED558065.pdf.

BU Center for Teaching and Learning. (2018). Active learning: Teaching guide. Retrieved from https://www.bu.edu/ctl/guides/active-learning/.

Burchard, B. (2006). *The student leadership guide*. Center for Leadership Development at the University of Montana.

Bush, T. (2011). *Theories of educational leadership & management* (4th ed). New York: Sage.

Butler, S., Urrutia, K., Buenger, A., Gonzalez, N., Hunt, M., & Eisenhart, C. (2010). A review of the current research on vocabulary instruction. Retrieved from https://www2.ed.gov/programs/readingfirst/support/rmcfinal1.pdf.

CAST. (2018). *UDL at a glance.* Retrieved from http://www.cast.org/our-work/about-udl.html#.WoBriOjwZPY.

Causton, J., & Theoharis, G. (2014). *The principal's handbook for leading inclusive schools.* Baltimore, MD: Brookes.

Cavell, T. A., & Elledge, L. C. (2014). Mentoring and prevention science. In D. L. DuBois & M. J. Karcher (Eds.), *Handbook of youth mentoring* (2nd ed., pp. 29–42). Thousand Oaks, CA: Sage.

Celli, L. M., & Young, N. D. (2014). *Learning style perspectives: Impact in the classroom* (3rd ed.). Madison, WI: Atwood.

Celtics. (2014). Read to achieve. Retrieved from http://www.nba.com/celtics/community/read_to_achieve.html.

Clarke, M. L. (1977). Bossuet and Fenelon as tutors to French royalty. *History Today, 27*(12), n.p. Retrieved from https://www.historytoday.com/ml-clarke/bossuet-and-fenelon-tutors-french-royalty.

Colker, L. (2014). The word gap: The early years make the difference. *Teaching Young Children, 7*(3). Retrieved from https://www.naeyc.org/resources/pubs/tyc/feb2014/the-word-gap.

College for Every Student. (n.d.). About us. Retrieved from http://www.collegefes.org/about-us/what-we-do.php.

Colorin Colorado. (2017). How to develop a lesson plan that includes ELLs. Retrieved from http://www.colorincolorado.org/article/how-develop-lesson-plan-includes-ells.

Connolly, M., & Giouroukakis, V. (2016). *Achieving next generation literacy.* Sterling, VA: ASCD.

Cook-Deegan, P. (2016). Seven ways to help high schoolers find purpose. *Greater Good Magazine.* Retrieved from https://greatergood.berkeley.edu/article/item/seven_ways_to_help_high_schoolers_find_purpose.

Cooper, M. S., Brown, C., Metzger, I., Clinton, Y., & Guthrie, B. (2012). Racial discrimination and African American adolescent's adjustment: Gender variation in family and community social support, promotive and protective factors. *Journal of Child & Family Studies, 22*, 15–29. doi:10.1007/s10826-012-9608-y.

Cowen, E., & Nee, M. (2016). 6 hand signals that bring learning to life. *Edutopia.* Retrieved from https://www.edutopia.org/blog/hand-signals-bring-learning-to-life-ellie-cowen.

Crippen, M. (2012). The value of children's literature. *Oneota Reading Journal.* Retrieved from https://www.luther.edu/oneota-reading-journal/archive/2012/the-value-of-childrens-literature/.

Dewey, J. (1963). *Experience and education.* New York: Collier Books.

Dirks, K. (2010). Bibliotherapy for the inclusive elementary classroom (Senior honors thesis, Eastern Michigan University, 2010). Retrieved from http://commons.emich.edu/cgi/viewcontent.cgi?article=1209&context=honors.

Donaldson, G. A. (2007) What do teachers bring to leadership? *Educational Leadership 65*(1), 26–29.

DuBois, D. L., & Karcher, M. J. (2013). Youth mentoring in contemporary perspective. In D. L. DuBois & M. J. Karcher (Eds.), *Handbook of youth mentoring* (pp. 3–14). Thousand Oaks, CA: Sage.

Dweck, C. (2007). *Mindset: The new psychology of success.* New York: Ballantine.

Elias, M. J. (2013a). Engaged teaching: "Do now" activities for your lessons. *Edutopia*. Retrieved from https://www.edutopia.org/blog/engaged-teaching-do-now-activities-sel-lessons-maurice-elias.

Elias, M. J. (2013b). Finding students' hidden strengths and passions. *Edutopia*. Retrieved from https://www.edutopia.org/blog/students-strengths-passions-maurice-elias.

Epstein, J. L. (2011). *School, family, and community partnerships: Preparing educators and improving schools* (2nd ed.). Boulder, CO: Westview Press.

Eye to Eye. (2018). Who we are. Retrieved from http://eyetoeyenational.org/.

Family Literacy (2015). Family literacy: What is family literacy? Retrieved from http://literacy.kent.edu/FamilyLiteracy/whatisit.html.

Ferlazzo, L. (2012). Cultivating student leadership. *Education Week Teacher*. Retrieved from https://www.edweek.org/tm/articles/2012/02/14/tln_ferlazzo_leadership.html.

Ferlazzo, L., & Hammond, L. A. (2009). *Building parent engagement in schools*. Santa Barbara, CA: Linworth.

Finley, T. (2014). Engage kids with 7 times the effect. *Edutopia*. Retrieved from https://www.edutopia.org/blog/engage-with-7x-the-effect-todd-finley.

Fishtree. (2017). 5 things you can do to support English language learners. Retrieved from https://www.fishtree.com/blog/5-things-you-can-do-to-support-english-language-learners.

Fletcher, A. (2017). Roles for students throughout the education system. *SoundOut*. Retrieved from https://soundout.org/roles-for-students-throughout-the-education-system/.

Foster, L. (2016). Building community with attendance questions. *Edutopia*. Retrieved from https://www.edutopia.org/blog/building-community-with-attendance-questions-lizanne-foster.

Gallagher, K. (2009). *Readicide: How schools are killing reading and what you can do about it*. Portland, ME: Stenhouse.

Gardner, H. E. (2011). *Frames of mind: The theory of multiple intelligences*. New York: Basic Books.

Garmezy, N., & Rutter, M. (1983). *Stress, coping, and development in children*. New York: McGraw-Hill.

Garringer, M., & MacRae, P. (2008). *Building effective peer mentoring services: An introductory guide*. Folsom, CA: Mentoring Resource Center.

Garringer, M., Kupersmidt, J., Rhodes, J., Stelter, R., & Tai, T. (2015). *Elements of effective practice for mentoring* (4th ed.). Boston, MA: MENTOR: The National Mentoring Partnership. Retrieved from https://www.mentoring.org/newsite/wpcontent/uploads/2015/09/FAQ_Elements_February2015.pdf.

Gavan, V. (2017). 5 ways to be an inclusive leader and build an inclusive culture. *CEO Magazine*. Retrieved from https://www.theceomagazine.com/business/5-ways-inclusive-leader-build-inclusive-culture.

Ginsberg, M. B. (2015). *Excited to learn: Motivation and culturally responsive teaching*. Thousand Oaks, CA: Corwin.

Gordon, J., Downey, J., & Bangert, A. (2013). Effects of a school-based mentoring program on school behavior and measures of adolescent connectedness. *School Community Journal*, 23(2), 227–249. Retrieved from https://eric.ed.gov/?id=EJ1028864.

Graham, S., & Hebert, M. A. (2010). *Writing to read: Evidence for how writing can improve reading: A Carnegie Corporation time to act report*. Washington, DC: Alliance for Excellent Education. Retrieved from https://www.carnegie.org/media/filer_public/9d/e2/9de20604-a055-42da-bc00-77da949b29d7/ccny_report_2010_writing.pdf.

Grant, K. B., & Ray, J. A. (2016). *Home, school, and community collaboration: Culturally responsive family engagement* (3rd ed.). Thousand Oaks, CA: Sage.

Greenleaf, R. K. (1977). *Servant leadership: A journey into the nature of legitimate power and greatness.* Mahwah, NJ: Paulist Press.

Greenleaf, R. K. (1998). The power of servant leadership. *Greenleaf Center for Servant Leadership.* San Francisco, CA: Berrett-Koehler.

Griffiths, D. (2013). *Principals of inclusion: Practical strategies to grow inclusion in urban schools.* Burlington, ON: Word & Deed.

Guroian, V. (2008). Literature and the real meaning of mentorship. Retrieved from https://www.baylor.edu/content/services/document.php/61114.pdf.

HarperCollins Publishers. (2018). D.E.A.R. Retrieved from http://dropeverythingandread.com/NationalDEARday.html.

Heath, R. (2016, Fall). Improving access to student leadership. *Washington Principal.* Retrieved from https://slidelegend.com/fall-2016-awsporg_5af7b2317f8b9afb1e8b458c.html.

Hirsch, J. (2014). Teaching empathy: Turning a lesson plan into a life skill. *Edutopia.* Retrieved from https://www.edutopia.org/blog/empathy-lesson-plan-life-skill-joe-hirsch.

Homer. (1996). *The odyssey.* (R. Fagles, Trans.). New York: Penguin Books. (Original work published 8th century BC.)

Houck, B. D., & Novak, S. (2016). *Literacy unleashed.* Alexandria, VA: ASCD.

Howard, S. (2016). Children and childhood. *African Studies.* doi:10.1093/OBO/9780199846733-0045.

Hull, G., & Schultz, K. (2002). *School's out: Bridging out-of-school literacies with classroom practice.* New York: Teachers College Press.

Hurd, N., & Sellers, R. M. (2013). Black adolescents' relationships with natural mentors. *Culturally Diverse Ethnic Minority Psychology, 19*(1), 76–85. doi:10.1037/a0031095.

Hurd, N., Varner, F., & Rowley, S. (2013). Involved-vigilant parenting and socio-emotional well-being among black youth: The moderating influence of natural mentoring relationships. *Journal of Youth and Adolescence, 42*(10), 1583–1595. doi:10.1007/s10964-012-9819-y.

Hurst, S. (2013). Seven ways to increase student engagement in the classroom. *Reading Horizons.* Retrieved from https://www.readinghorizons.com/blog/seven-ways-to-increase-student-engagement-in-the-classroom.

International Literacy Association. (2018). *International literacy day.* Retrieved from https://www.literacyworldwide.org/meetings-events/international-literacy-day.

Ivey, G., & Broaddus, K. (2001). "Just plain reading": A survey of what makes students want to read in middle school. *Reading Research Quarterly, 36*(4), 350–377. Retrieved from https://eric.ed.gov/?id=EJ634592.

Jacobsen, L. (2014). Why boys don't read. *Great Schools.* Retrieved from http://www.greatschools.org/students/academic-skills/6832-why-so-many-boys-do-not-read.gs.

Jensen, E. (2005). *Learning with the brain in mind* (2nd ed.). Alexandria, VA: ASCD.

Jensen, E. (2013). How poverty affects classroom engagement. *Educational Leadership, 70*(8), 24–30. Retrieved from http://www.ascd.org/publications/educational-leadership/may13/vol70/num08/How-Poverty-Affects-Classroom-Engagement.aspx.

Johnson, B. (2018). A recipe for inspiring life-long learning. *Edutopia.* Retrieved from https://www.edutopia.org/article/recipe-inspiring-lifelong-learning.

Johnson, D. W., & Johnson, R. T. (2004). An overview of cooperative learning. *Cooperative Learning.* Retrieved from http://www.co-operation.org/what-is-cooperative-learning/.

Johnson, D. W., Johnson, R. T., & Holubec, E. J. (2008). *Cooperation in the classroom: Revised* (8th ed.). Edina, MN: Interaction Book Co.

Jucovy, L., & Garringer, M. (2008). *The ABCs of school-based mentoring*. Washington, DC: Hamilton Fish Institute on School and Community Violence and National Mentoring Center. Retrieved from http://educationnorthwest.org/sites/default/files/abcs-of-mentoring.pdf.

Karcher, M. J. (2013). Cross-age peer mentoring. In D. L. DuBois & M. J. Karcher (Eds.), *Handbook of youth mentoring* (pp. 233–257). Thousand Oaks, CA: Sage.

Kittle, P. (2013). *Book love: Developing depth, stamina, and passion in adolescent readers*. Portsmouth, NH: Heinemann.

Klein, A. (2016). The Every Student Succeeds Act: An overview. *Education Week*. Retrieved from https://www.edweek.org/ew/issues/every-student-succeeds-act/index.html.

Kohut, H. (1977). *Restoration of the self*. New York: International Universities Press.

Komosa-Hawkins, K. (2010). Best practices in school-based mentoring programs for adolescents. *Child & Youth Services, 31*(3–4), 121–137. Retrieved from https://eric.ed.gov/?id=EJ929688.

Korbey, H. (2016). How to develop a love of reading. *KQED*. Retrieved from https://www.kqed.org/mindshift/46501/how-to-help-students-develop-a-love-of-reading.

Kouzes, J. M., & Posner, B. Z. (2014). *The student leadership challenge: Five practices of exemplary student leadership*. San Francisco, CA: Jossey-Bass.

Kroger, J. (2007). *Identity development: Adolescence through adulthood*. Thousand Oaks, CA: Sage.

Kuperminc, G. P., & Thomason, J. D. (2014). Group mentoring. In D. L. DuBois & M. J. Karcher (Eds.), *Handbook of youth mentoring* (2nd ed., pp. 273–289). Thousand Oaks, CA: Sage.

Larmer, J. (2016). Gold standard PBL: Student voice and choice. *PBL Blog*. Retrieved from https://www.bie.org/blog/gold_standard_pbl_student_voice_choice.

Larmer, J., Mergendoller, J., & Boss, S. (2015). *Setting the standard for project-based learning: A proven approach to rigorous classroom instruction*. Alexandria, VA: ASCD.

Laviolette, J. L. (2016). 7 great ways to give back by promoting literacy at your business. *Groupon Merchant Business*. Retrieved from www.groupon.com/merchant/blog/ways-to-give-back-promote-literacy-business.

Lemov, D. (2015). *Teach like a champion 2.0*. San Francisco, CA: Jossey-Bass.

Lerner, R. M., Napolitano, C. M., Boyd, M. J., Mueller, M. K., & Callina, K. S. (2014). Mentoring and positive youth development. In D. L. DuBois & M. J. Karcher (Eds.), *Handbook of youth mentoring* (2nd ed., pp. 17–28). Thousand Oaks, CA: Sage.

Liang, B., Bogat, A., & Duffy, N. (2013). Gender in mentoring relationships. In D. L. DuBois & M. J. Karcher (Eds.), *Handbook of youth mentoring* (pp. 159–174). Thousand Oaks, CA: Sage.

Liao, L. C., & Sanchez, B. (2015). An exploratory study of the role of mentoring in the acculturation of Latino/a youth. *Journal of Community Psychology, 43*(7), 868–877.

Lindsay, S., Hartman, L., & Fellin, M. (2016). A systematic review of mentorship programs to facilitate transition to post-secondary education and employment for youth and young adults with disabilities. *Disability and Rehabilitation, 38*(14). doi:10.3109/09638288.2015.1092174.

Lopez, R. (2012). Teachers as mentors for students "at risk" (PowerPoint presentation). Retrieved from http://webcache.googleusercontent.com/search?q=cache:lxNaP7hssRoJ:images.pcmac.org/Uploads/NeshobaCounty/NeshobaCounty/Departments/DocumentsCategories/Documents/Teachers%2520as%2520Mentors%2520for%2520Students%2520At-%2520Risk%2520PPt.pptx+&cd=2&hl=en&ct=clnk&gl=us.

Mader, J. (2017). How teacher training hinders special-needs students. *Atlantic*. Retrieved from https://www.theatlantic.com/education/archive/2017/03/how-teacher-training-hinders-special-needs-students/518286/.

Major, S. K. (2016). Teaching strategies that meet the needs of kinesthetic learners. *Child 1st*. Retrieved from https://child1st.com/blogs/resources/113159303-teaching-strategies-that-meet-the-needs-of-kinesthetic-learners.

Mapp, K. L., & Kuttner, P. J. (2013). Partners in education: A dual capacity-building framework for family-school partnerships. Retrieved from http://www.sedl.org/pubs/framework/FE-Cap-Building.pdf.

Martin, A. (2011). Teachers as mentors for students. *Morningside Center*. Retrieved from http://www.morningsidecenter.org/teachable-moment/lessons/teacher-mentors-students.

Martinez, M. (2014). 6 rules to break for better, deeper-learning outcomes. *Edutopia*. Retrieved from https://www.edutopia.org/blog/rules-to-break-deeper-learning-monica-martinez.

Marzano, R. J., & Pickering, D. J. (2011). *The highly engaged classroom*. Bloomington, IN: Marzano Research Laboratory.

Maslow, A. H. (1968). *Toward a psychology of being* (2nd ed.). Princeton, NJ: Van Nostrand Reinhold.

Maslow, A. H. (2013). *A theory of human motivation* (Reprint of 1943 edition). Eastford, CT: Martino Fine Books.

Mastropieri, M. A., & Scruggs, T. E. (2018). *The inclusive classroom: Strategies for effective differentiated instruction* (6th ed). Boston: Prentice Hall.

McCarthy, J. (2015). Igniting student engagement: A roadmap for learning. *Edutopia*. Retrieved from https://www.edutopia.org/blog/ignite-student-engagement-roadmap-learning-john-mccarthy.

McCoy, R. L. (2017). Best practices for school-based mentoring programs: A systematic review. *Master of Social Work Clinical Research Papers, 766*. Retrieved from https://sophia.stkate.edu/cgi/viewcontent.cgi?article=1767&context=msw_papers.

McDonald, J. P., Smith, S., Turner, D., Finney, M., & Barton, E. (1993). *Graduation by exhibition: Assessing genuine achievement*. Alexandria, VA: ASCD.

McLeskey, J. (2011). Supporting improved practice for special education teachers: The importance of learner-centered professional development. *Journal of Special Education Leadership, 24*(1), 26–35. Retrieved from https://eric.ed.gov/?id=EJ926849.

Michael, C. (2006). *Multiple ways of being a CFES leader*. www.collegefes.org.

Michael, C., & McKibben, S. (2006). And a child shall lead them. Report to Foundation for Excellent Schools. Unpublished manuscript.

Milsom, A. (2017). Creating positive school experience for students with disabilities. *Reading Rockets*. Retrieved from http://www.readingrockets.org/article/creating-positive-school-experiences-students-disabilities.

Mizell, H. (2010). Why professional development matters. Retrieved from https://learningforward.org/docs/default-source/pdf/why_pd_matters_web.pdf.

Morrison, K. A. (2008). Democratic classrooms: Promises and challenges of student voice and choice, part one. *Educational Horizons*, 50–60. Retrieved from https://files.eric.ed.gov/fulltext/EJ815371.pdf.

Murphy, D. (2012). Reading challenges. *From Mrs. Murphy's Desk*. Retrieved from http://motivatingmiddleschoolstudents.blogspot.com.

Nagro, S. A., Hooks, S. D., Fraser, D. W., and Cornelius, K. E. (2016). Whole-group response strategies to promote student engagement in inclusive classrooms. *Teaching Exceptional Children, 48*(5), 243–249. doi:10.1177/0040059916640749.

The National Center for Families Learning. (2018). Our why. Retrieved from http://www.familieslearning.org/our-why/about-NCFL.html.

National Center for Learning Disabilities. (n.d.). Home literacy environment checklist. Retrieved from http://www.reachoutandread.org/FileRepository/HomeLiteracyChecklist.pdf.

National Education Association. (2017). *Background on Read across America.* Retrieved from http://www.nea.org/grants/read-across-background.html.

National Endowment for the Arts. (2004). Reading at risk: A survey of literary reading in America. Research Division Report #46. Retrieved from https://www.arts.gov/sites/default/files/ReadingAtRisk.pdf.

National Federation of State High School Associations. (2018). The case for high school activities. Retrieved from https://www.nfhs.org/articles/the-case-for-high-school-activities/.

National Urban Fellows. (2018). About us. Retrieved from http://www.nuf.org/mission-vision.

New York Life Foundation. (2007). Leadership through service: Our time to serve, our turn to lead. Retrieved from www.collegefes.org.

Newcomb, T., & Michael, C. (2010). Our time to serve, our turn to lead. Monograph, New York Life Insurance. Unpublished manuscript. Cornwall, VT: College for Every Student.

Niemiec, C. P. & Ryan, R. M. (2009). Autonomy, competence, and relatedness: Applying self-determination theory to educational practice. *Theory and Research in Education 7*(2), 133–144. doi:10.1177/1477878509104318.

Northouse, P. G. (2018). Leadership theory and practice (8th ed.). Los Angeles, CA: Sage.

Norton, D. E., & Norton, S. (2011). *Through the eyes of a child: An introduction to children's literature.* Boston: Pearson.

Oberoi, A. K. (2016). Mentoring for first-generation immigrant and refugee youth. *National Mentoring Resource Center.* Retrieved from https://nationalmentoringresourcecenter.org/index.php/what-works-in-mentoring/model-and-population-reviews.html?id=228.

Palmer, P. J. (2007). *The courage to teach: Exploring the inner landscape of a teacher's life.* San Francisco: Jossey-Bass.

Pino-James, N. (2014). Golden rules for engaging students in learning activities. *Edutopia.* Retrieved from https://www.edutopia.org/blog/golden-rules-for-engaging-students-nicolas-pino-james.

PPEP Tec. (2016). How students benefit from participating in school sports. Retrieved from http://www.ppeptechs.org/642.

Probst, K. (2006). *Mentoring for meaningful results.* Minneapolis: Search Institute.

Provenzano, N. (2016). 4 practices for increasing student engagement. *Edutopia.* Retrieved from https://www.edutopia.org/blog/practices-for-increasing-student-engagement-nicholas-provenzano.

Quick, T., Hocevar, D., & Zimmer, M. (2014). *Making reading relevant: The art of connecting.* New York: Pearson Education.

Ragsdale, S. (2014). 8 play-based strategies to engage youth in learning. *Edutopia.* Retrieved from https://www.edutopia.org/blog/play-based-strategies-engage-leaning-susan-ragsdale.

Rawls, W. (1961). *Where the red fern grows.* New York: Penguin Random House.

Reader to Reader. (n.d.). About us. Retrieved from http://www.readertoreader.org/about.

Reading Recovery. (2018). Basic facts. Retrieved from https://readingrecovery.org/reading-recovery/teaching-children/basic-facts/.

Reeve, J. (2006). Teachers as facilitators: What autonomy-supportive teachers do and why their students benefit. *Elementary School Journal 106*(3), 225–236. doi:10.1086/501484.

Reid, K. S. (2014). School districts get advice on "doing more with less." *Education Week.* Retrieved from https://www.edweek.org/ew/articles/2014/05/07/30savings.h33.html.

Rhodes, J. (2015). Top 25 mentoring relationships in history. *Chronicle of Evidence-Based Learning.* Retrieved from https://chronicle.umbmentoring.org/top-25-mentoring-relationships-in-history/.

Rhodes, J. E. (2002). *Stand by me: The risks and rewards of mentoring today's youth.* Cambridge, MA: Harvard University Press.

Robertson, D. (2016). Inclusive leadership. Retrieved from https://marshallelearning.com/wp-content/uploads/2016/11/Inclusive-Leadership-Whitepaper-1.pdf.

Robertson, K. (2014). Five things teachers can do to improve learning for ELLs in the New Year. *Colorín Colorado.* Retrieved from http://www.colorincolorado.org/article/five-things-teachers-can-do-improve-learning-ells-new-year.

Rosen, P. (2018). MTSS: What you need to know. *Understood.* Retrieved from https://www.understood.org/en/learning-attention-issues/treatments-approaches/educational-strategies/mtss-what-you-need-to-know.

Rotich, J. (2011) Mentoring as a springboard to acculturation of immigrant students into American Schools. *Journal of Case Studies in Education.* Retrieved from https://files.eric.ed.gov/fulltext/EJ1055522.pdf.

Routman, R. (2014). *Read, write, lead: Breakthrough strategies for schoolwide literacy success.* Alexandria, VA: ASCD.

Ryan, J. (2006). *Inclusive leadership.* San Francisco: Jossey-Bass.

Ryan, R. M., & Deci, E. L. (2000). Self-determination theory and the facilitation of intrinsic motivation, social development, and well-being. *American Psychologist 55*(1), 68–78. Retrieved from https://selfdeterminationtheory.org/SDT/documents/2000_RyanDeci_SDT.pdf.

Saint Joseph's University. (2018). Creative ways to engage special education students. Retrieved from https://online.sju.edu/graduate/masters-special-education/resources/articles/six-creative-ways-to-engage-special-education-students.

Samuels, C. A. (2016). ESSA spotlights strategy to reach diverse learners. *Education Week.* Retrieved from https://www.edweek.org/ew/articles/2016/02/24/essa-spotlights-strategy-to-reach-diverse-learners.html.

Scholastic. (2014). *Kids and family reading report* (5th ed). Retrieved from http://www.scholastic.com/readingreport/Scholastic-KidsAndFamilyReadingReport-5thEdition.pdf?v=100.

Scholastic. (2015). 17 ways to keep your middle schooler turning the pages. Retrieved from www.scholastic.com/parents/resources/article/more-reading-resources/17-ways-to-keep-your-middle-schooler-turning-the-pages.

Scholastic. (2018). Read and rise. Retrieved from http://teacher.scholastic.com/products/face/read-and-rise.html.

Schwartz, S. E. O., Rhodes, J. E., Chan, C. S., & Herrera, C. (2011). The impact of school-based mentoring on youths with different relational profiles. *Developmental Psychology, 47*(2), 450–462. doi:10.1037/a0021379.

Shabiralyani, G., Hasan, K. S., Hamad, N., & Iqbal, N. (2015). Impact of visual aids in enhancing the learning process. *Journal of Education and Practice, 6*(19). Retrieved from https://files.eric.ed.gov/fulltext/EJ1079541.pdf.

Shambaugh, R. (2017). What inclusive leaders do. *Huffington Post.* Retrieved from https://www.huffingtonpost.com/entry/what-inclusive-leaders-do_us_59663caee4b09be48c0056c5.

Shea, G. F. (1997). *Mentoring.* Menlo Park CA: Crisp.

Sheehy, G. (1986). *Spirit of survival.* New York: William Morrow.

Shpigelman, C.-N. (2013). Electronic mentoring and media. In D. L. DuBois & M. J. Karcher (Eds.), *Handbook of youth mentoring* (pp. 259–272). Thousand Oaks, CA: Sage.

Shrodes, C. (1955). Bibliotherapy. *Reading Teacher, 9*, 24–30. Retrieved from http://jstor.org/stable/20196879.

Simoes, F. (2014). Teachers as school-based mentors for at-risk students: A qualitative study. *Child & Youth Care Forum, 43*(1), 113–133. doi:10.1007/s10566-013-9228-8.

Sinha, K. (2014). Kinesthetic learning: Moving toward a new model for education. *Edutopia*. Retrieved from https://www.edutopia.org/blog/kinesthetic-learning-new-model-education-kirin-sinha.

Six Flags. (2017). Read to succeed. Retrieved from https://www.sixflags.com/greatamerica/community.

Slavin, R. E. (1996). Research on cooperative learning and achievement: What we know, what we need to know. *Contemporary Educational Psychology, 21*(1), 43–69. DOI: 10.1006/ceps.1996.0004.

Smith, M. W., & Wilhelm, J. D. (2002). *Reading don't fix no Chevys: Literacy in the lives of young men.* Portsmouth, NH: Heinemann.

Smith, M. W., & Wilhelm, J. D. (2006). *Going with the flow: How to engage boys (and girls) in their literacy learning.* Portsmouth, NH: Heinemann.

Southwest Educational Development Laboratory. (2005). Reaching our reading goals. *SEDL Letter.* Retrieved from http://www.sedl.org/pubs/sedl-letter/v17n01/SEDLLetter_v17n01.pdf.

Spear-Swerling, L. (2006). Vocabulary assessment and instruction for students with learning disabilities. *Reading Rockets.* Retrieved from http://www.readingrockets.org/article/vocabulary-assessment-and-instruction-students-learning-disabilities.

Spray, A. (2015). The science of why music improves our memory and verbal intelligence. *Washington Post.* Retrieved from https://www.washingtonpost.com/posteverything/wp/2015/07/21/the-science-of-why-music-improves-our-memory-and-verbal-intelligence/?utm_term=.a8af2b1d47ae.

Spring, K., Dietz, N., & Grimm, R. (2006). *Educating for active citizenship: Service-learning, school-based service, and civic engagement.* Corporation for National and Community Service.

Stephens, T. (2015). Encouraging positive student engagement and motivation: Tips for teachers. *Pearson.* Retrieved from https://www.pearsoned.com/encouraging-positive-student-engagement-and-motivation-tips-for-teachers/.

Stuber, N. (2014). *Nutrition and students' academic performance.* Retrieved from https://www.wilder.org/Wilder-Research/Publications/Studies/Fueling%20Academic%20Performance%20-%20Strategies%20to%20Foster%20Healthy%20Eating%20Among%20Students/Nutrition%20and%20Students'%20Academic%20Performance.pdf.

Success for All Foundation. (2015). Our approach. Retrieved from http://www.successforall.org/our-approach/.

Sztabnik, B. (2015). The 8 minutes that matter most. *Edutopia.* Retrieved from https://www.edutopia.org/blog/8-minutes-that-matter-most-brian-sztabnik.

Tatum, A. (2005). *Teaching reading to black adolescent males: Closing the achievement gap.* Portland, ME: Stenhouse.

TeachThought. (2018). 25 ways schools can promote literacy and independent reading. Retrieved from https://www.teachthought.com/literacy/25-ways-schools-can-promote-literacy-independent-reading/.

Thompson, J. (2015). Supporting student engagement for students with IEPs. Retrieved from http://msuk12connect.org/articles/achievement-gaps/222-supporting-student-engagement-for-students-with-ieps.

Tinto, V. (1993). *Leaving college: Rethinking the causes and cures for student attrition.* Chicago: University of Chicago Press.

Tomlinson, C. A. (2015). Differentiation does, in fact, work. *Education Week.* Retrieved from https://www.edweek.org/ew/articles/2015/01/28/differentiation-does-in-fact-work.html.

Tracey, D., Hornery, S., Seaton, M., Craven, R. G., & Yeung, A. S. (2014). Volunteers supporting children with reading difficulties in schools: Motives and rewards. *School Community Journal, 24*(1), 49–68. Retrieved from https://eric.ed.gov/?id=EJ1032241.

Tu, W. (1999). Using literature to help children cope with problems. *ERIC Clearinghouse on Reading English and Communication.* Retrieved from https://files.eric.ed.gov/fulltext/ED436008.pdf.

University of Maryland. (2018). Jump Start 2018. Retrieved from http://hhmi.umd.edu/jumpstart/.

University of Washington. (2018). Engaging students in learning. Retrieved from http://www.washington.edu/teaching/teaching-resources/engaging-students-in-learning/https://www2.ed.gov/policy/gen/guid/secletter/productivity.doc.

van Linden, J. A., & Fertman, C. I. (1998). *Youth leadership: A guide to understanding leadership development in adolescents.* San Francisco: Jossey-Bass.

Vygotsky, L. (1962). *Thought and language.* Cambridge, MA: MIT Press.

Wallin, D. (2003). Student leadership and democratic schools: A case study. *NASSP Bulletin 87*(636), 55–78. doi:10.1177/019263650308763606.

Weiser, B. (2014). Academic diversity: Ways to motivate and engage students with learning disabilities. *Council for Learning Disabilities.* Retrieved from https://council-for-learning-disabilities.org/wp-content/uploads/2014/07/Weiser_Motivation.pdf.

Wentzel, K. (2015). Prosocial behavior and schooling. *Encyclopedia on Early Childhood Development.* Retrieved from http://www.child-encyclopedia.com/prosocial-behaviour/according-experts/prosocial-behaviour-and-schooling.

Werner, E. E., & Smith, R. S. (1992). *Overcoming the odds: High risk children from birth to adulthood.* Ithaca, NY: Cornell University Press.

WGBH Educational Foundation. (2002). Where do I begin? *PBS.* Retrieved from http://www.pbs.org/wgbh/misunderstoodminds/readingstrats.html.

Wiener, H. S. (1988). *Talk with your child.* New York: Viking.

Wiggins, G., & McTighe, J. (2011). *Understanding by design: Guide to creating high-quality units.* Alexandria, VA: ASCD.

Wise Guys. (2017). Using growth mindset to increase student engagement {Tips for the upper elementary teacher!}. Retrieved from http://www.creativityinthemodernclassroom.com/2017/02/using-growth-mindset-to-increase-student-engagement/.

Wolpert-Gawron, H. (2018). *Just ask us: Kids speak out on student engagement.* Thousand Oaks, CA: Corwin.

Wood, J. (2016). Reading stamina: What is it? Can I plan for it? *NWEA.* Retrieved from https://www.nwea.org/blog/2016/reading-stamina-what-is-it-can-i-plan-for-it/.

Wood, S., & Mayo-Wilson, E. (2012). School-based mentoring for adolescents: A systematic review and meta-analysis. *Research on Social Work Practice, 22*(3), 257–269. doi:10.1177/1049731511430836.

Woods, C., & Preciado, M. (2016). Student–mentor relationships and students' college attitudes. *Journal of Education for Students Placed at Risk, 21*(2), 90–103. doi:10.100/1024669.2015.1127767.

Young, N. D., Bonanno-Sotiropoulos, K., & Smolinski, J. A. (2018). *Guardians of the next generation: Igniting the passion for high-quality teaching.* New York: Rowman & Littlefield.

Young, N. D., & Jean, E. (2018). There's an app for that: Teaching with technology in mind. In N. D. Young, E. Jean, & T. A. Citro (Eds.), *Stars in the schoolhouse: Teaching practices and approaches that make a difference.* Wilmington, DE: Vernon Press.

Young, N. D., Jean, E., & Mead, A. E. (2018). *From cradle to classroom: A guide to special education for our youngest children.* Wilmington, DE: Vernon Press.

Young, N. D., Jean (Bienia), E., & Quayson, F. (2017). *From lecture hall to laptop: Opportunities, challenges, and the continuing evolution of virtual learning in higher education.* Madison, IL: Atwood.

Young, N. D., & Michael, C. N. (2015). *Beyond the bedtime story: Promoting reading development during the middle school years.* Lanham, MD: Rowman & Littlefield.

Young, N. D., Noonan, B. T., & Bonanno-Sotiropoulos, K. (2018). *Wrestling with writing: Effective instructional strategies for struggling students.* New York: Rowman & Littlefield.

About the Authors

Nicholas D. Young, PhD, EdD, has worked in diverse educational roles for more than 30 years as a principal, special education director, graduate professor, graduate program director, graduate dean, and longtime superintendent of schools. He was named the Massachusetts Superintendent of the Year and completed a distinguished Fulbright program focused on the Japanese educational system through the collegiate level. Dr. Young is the recipient of numerous other honors and recognitions, including the General Douglas MacArthur Award for distinguished civilian and military leadership and the Vice Admiral John T. Hayward Award for exemplary scholarship. He holds several graduate degrees, including a PhD in educational administration and an EdD in educational psychology.

Dr. Young has served in the U.S. Army and U.S. Army Reserves, combined, for more than 34 years and graduated with distinction from the U.S. Air War College, the U.S. Army War College, and the U.S. Navy War College. After completing a series of senior leadership assignments in the U.S. Army Reserves as the commanding officer of the 287th Medical Company (DS), the 405th Area Support Company (DS), the 405th Combat Support Hospital, and the 399th Combat Support Hospital, he transitioned to his current military position as a faculty instructor at the U.S. Army War College in Carlisle, PA. He currently holds the rank of colonel.

Dr. Young is also a regular presenter at state, national, and international conferences and has written many books, book chapters, and articles on various topics in education, counseling, and psychology. Some of his most recent books are *Securing the Schoolyard, Protocols that Promote Safety and*

Positive Student Behaviors (at press); *Sounding the Alarm in the Schoolhouse: Safety, Security, and Student Well-Being* (at press); *The Soul of the Schoolhouse: Cultivating Student Engagement* (2019); *Embracing and Educating the Autistic Child: Valuing Those Who Color Outside the Lines* (2019); *Potency of the Principalship: Action-Oriented Leadership at the Heart of School Improvement* (2018); *Soothing the Soul: Pursuing a Life of Abundance through a Practice of Gratitude* (2018); *Stars in the Schoolhouse: Teaching Practices and Approaches That Make a Difference* (2018); *Guardian of the Next Generation: Igniting the Passion for Quality Teaching* (2018); *From Head to Heart: High-Quality Teaching Practices in the Spotlight* (2018); *Dog Tags to Diploma: Understanding and Addressing the Educational Needs of Veterans, Servicemembers, and Their Families* (2018); *From Cradle to Classroom: A Guide to Special Education for Young Children* (2018); *Achieving Results: Maximizing Success in the Schoolhouse* (2018); *Making the Grade: Promoting Positive Outcomes for Students with Learning Disabilities* (2018); *Paving the Pathway for Educational Success: Effective Classroom Interventions for Students with Learning Disabilities* (2018); *Wrestling with Writing: Effective Strategies for Struggling Students* (2018); *Floundering to Fluent: Reaching and Teaching the Struggling Student* (2018); *Emotions and Education: Promoting Positive Mental Health in Students with Learning* (2018); *From Lecture Hall to Laptop: Opportunities, Challenges, and the Continuing Evolution of Virtual Learning in Higher Education* (2017); *The Power of the Professoriate: Demands, Challenges, and Opportunities in 21st-Century Higher Education* (2017); and *To Campus with Confidence: Supporting a Successful Transition to College for Students with Learning Disabilities* (2017). He also coauthored several children's books in the popular series I Am Full of Possibilities. Dr. Young may be contacted at nyoung1191@aol.com.

Christine N. Michael, PhD, is an educational veteran of more than 40 years, with a variety of professional experiences. She holds degrees from Brown University, Rhode Island College, Union Institute and University, and the University of Connecticut, where she earned a PhD in education, human development, and family relations. Her previous work has included middle and high school teaching, higher education administration, college teaching, and educational consulting. She has also been involved with Head Start, Upward Bound, national nonprofits Foundation for Excellent Schools and College for Every Student, and the federal Trio programs, and she has published widely on topics in education and psychology. She is the author of *Securing the Schoolyard: Protocols that Promote Safety and Positive Student Behaviors* (at press); *Sounding the Alarm in the Schoolhouse: Safety, Security, and Student Well-Being* (at press); *The Soul of the Schoolhouse: Cultivating Student Engagement* (2019); *Turbulent Times: Confronting Challenges in Emerging Adulthood* (2018); and *To Campus with Confidence: Supporting a Successful Transition to College for Students with Learning Disabilities* (2017). She is the program director of low-residency programs at American International College. Dr. Michael may be contacted at cnevadam@gmail.com.

Jennifer A. Smolinski, attorney, has worked in education for more than three years. She created and directed the Center for Disability Services and Academic Accommodations at American International College in Springfield, MA. She has also taught criminal justice and legal research and writing classes within the field of higher education. Prior to her work at the collegiate level, she worked as a solo practitioner conducting education and disability advocacy, as well as representing clients in real estate and business matters.

Ms. Smolinski received a BA in anthropology and BA in sociology from the University of Connecticut, a master's in psychology and counseling and master's in higher education student affairs from Salem State University, and a law degree from the Massachusetts School of Law. She is an EdD in educational leadership and supervision candidate at American International College, where she is focused on special education and laws to protect students with disabilities in the classroom.

Ms. Smolinski has become a regular presenter, educating the faculty, staff, and students at institutes of higher education on disabilities and accommodations at the collegiate level, and has presented to local high school special education departments on the transition to college under the Americans with Disabilities Act. She coauthored *Securing the Schoolyard, Protocols that Promote Safety and Positive Student Behaviors* (at press); *Sounding the Alarm in the Schoolhouse: Safety, Security, and Student Well-Being* (at press); *Guardian of the Next Generation: Igniting the Passion for Quality Teaching* (at press), *Paving the Pathway for Educational Success: Effective Classroom Interventions for Students with Learning Disabilities* (2018), and *Making the Grade: Promoting Positive Outcomes for Students with Learning Disabilities* (2018). She can be reached at jennifer.smolinski@aic.edu.

www.ingramcontent.com/pod-product-compliance
Lightning Source LLC
Chambersburg PA
CBHW021845220426
43663CB00005B/408